SURTEES · JIM CLARK · JACKIE STEW

HUNT · NIGEL MANSEL   N

GRAHAM HILL · STIR

BELL · GERRY MARSHALL · JAMES H

FRANCHITTI · LEWIS HAMILTON · GR

CLARK · JACKIE STEWART · DEREK B

SELL · MARTIN BRUNDLE · DARIO FR

RLING MOSS · JOHN SURTEES · JIM C

ALL · JAMES HUNT · NIGEL MANSELL

HAMILTON · GRAHAM HILL · STIRLI

EWART · DEREK BELL · GERRY MARSH

NDLE · DARIO FRANCHITTI · LEWIS

SURTEES · JIM CLARK · JACKIE STEV

NIGEL MANSELL · MARTIN BRUND

AM HILL · STIRLING MOSS · JOHN S

BELL · GERRY MARSHALL · JAMES HU

FRANCHITTI · LEWIS HAMILTON · GR

CLARK · JACKIE STEWART · DEREK B

SELL · MARTIN BRUNDLE · DARIO FR

RLING MOSS · JOHN SURTEES · JIM

ALL · JAMES HUNT · NIGEL MANSELL

HAMILTON · GRAHAM HILL · STIRL

The

IMMORTALS

of British Motor Racing

The

IMMORTALS

— *of* British Motor Racing —

David Addison

A Gelding Street Press book
An imprint of Rockpool Publishing
PO Box 252, Summer Hill, NSW 2130, Australia
www.geldingstreetpress.com

ISBN: 9781922662019

Published in 2024 by Rockpool Publishing

IMAGE CREDITS

British Racing Drivers Club: ii, 10, 11, 24, 30, 31, 32, 37, 41, 43, 51, 52, 54, 56, 58, 60, 65, 84, 86, 89, 95, 97, 100, 105, 106, 109, 110, 112, 117, 118, 120, 126, 127, 178 • Alamy: vi, viii, 2, 6, 14, 17, 18, 25, 44, 74, 77, 98, 124, 129, 131, 137, 140, 143, 152, 182 • Classic Team Lotus (PR): 3 • John Morris: 4 • Ford (PR): 9, 46, 48, 66, 69, 70, 102 • Autosport International (PR): 13, 34, 38, 45, 57, 63, 115,172, 173 • Mercedes-Benz (PR): 21, 22, 150, 155, 156, 159, 160, 161, 162, 163 • Brooklands Museum (PR): 26, 29, • Concours D'Elegance (PR): 71 • Porsche (PR): 72, 78, 81, 82, 83, 166, 167 • Vauxhall (PR): 90, 92, 93 • Silverstone Classic (PR): 107 • Newspix: 116 • IndyCar (PR): 121 • Photographer unknown: 132 • Nissan (PR): 135 • London Classic Car Show (PR): 138 • Lexus (PR): 144 • Honda Racing (PR): 147 • Shutterstock: 148 • Renault (PR): 153 • Public domain: 164, 165 • McLaren Automotive (PR): 168, 175 • Gaucho Productions (PR): 169 • FIA (PR): 171 • Audi Motorsport (PR): 174

Design and typesetting by Christine Armstrong, Rockpool Publishing
Acquisition editor: Luke West, Rockpool Publishing
Edited by Brooke Halliwell

A catalogue record for this book is available from the National Library of Australia

Printed and bound in China

10 9 8 7 6 5 4 3 2 1

DEDICATION

For motor racing fans, old and new

CONTENTS

Two legends of the sport and proud members of the British Racing Drivers' Club, Stirling Moss and Jackie Stewart, whose abilities prevailed in a less commercial world.

INTRODUCTION

When an email arrives from someone saying that they have had an idea, the temptation often is to grin and hope they forget whatever brainwave by which they had been exercised. But just sometimes . . .

The Immortals series has been a popular concept in Australia covering heroes of a variety of sports and the suggestion that an equivalent motor racing title be written in the UK was an exciting one, yet daunting. After all, many books have been written about a number of the people contained within these covers. Equally, how do we decide what makes someone an immortal figure?

Immortality is an imprecise mix of fame, prodigious talent, competitive success, remarkable achievement and magnetism. One does not need to tick all of these boxes to be considered an immortal. For instance, being a household name – to coin a phrase that's not as widely used today as in the past – is a very good start. But it's not the be-all-and-end-all of immortality as there are legendary figures who caused a significant shift in the way their chosen sport was played or approached, who never reached the dizzying heights of others in competition.

I don't expect you to agree with all of my choices, argue as you wish, but what I have tried to do is focus on 12 drivers who have made an impact on the sport through a variety of means. After all, the biggest cop-out would be just to have written about Britain's F1 world champions, but that sells many others short.

Actually, what initially seemed like an easy task of writing 12 chapters soon became the topic of much debate. Australian journalist-turned-publisher Luke West, my old friend who approached me with this idea, posed the question as to whether we should limit ourselves to just English Immortals, although we both decided that an omission of two Scottish world champions may well start a revolt. Do we look at motorsport or just motor racing? Again, we settled on racing and hence there remains scope for debate on Great Britain's top rally drivers. Or motorcycle racing? Or even stock car racing,

Two successful racers and great characters from an age where a driver was allowed a personality. Gerry Marshall and James Hunt enjoy a drink together.

a branch of the sport with a die-hard fan base and committed drivers happy to plunge into bash-and-crash combat every weekend. What about those people who have made an outstanding contribution off-track? Aerodynamicists, technical directors, constructors, team owners . . . That is a book in itself. Eventually, we settled on 12 of Britain's best drivers. Ah, but which 12? Then the hard work really started.

Some of our Immortals are no longer with us but their memory lives on either by their achievements or through trophies awarded annually in their honour. Many are still talked about today and that, crucially, gives them a head start in my opinion because while results are one thing, it is a driver's contribution to the sport that adds weight for our purposes. We can look at drivers' statistics all day long, but it is hardly a fair comparison as times change. Look at a Formula 1 season, for example. From just six races in 1950 when the world championship started to 23 races slated for 2023, albeit one was lost to weather. In other words, you can make statistics tell you anything

Jim Clark's death in 1968 robbed the sport of a huge talent and left unanswered the question of how much more he could have achieved.

With a social media profile like no other driver's, Lewis Hamilton has attracted fans from outside the sport and has remained an outspoken champion of social issues to the admiration of many.

you want and nor do they take into account the level of opposition to a driver in a given era or the dominance or otherwise of a car or team. You can be the driver to beat one season and be struggling the next and it is oh-so easy to dismiss a driver based on results alone. I confess to loving long-distance racing in which so much can happen and yet drivers can get lost in the results of such races. In a world where the proliferation of pro-am races has boomed, there is gainful employment for guns for hire with a wealthy and enthusiastic amateur. But pair with a slow amateur and it spells trouble as you slide down the results sheet and a driver's individual contribution is ignored.

Rule changes, team personnel changes, weather . . . there are so many factors that can contribute to a driver's results and reputation. This is one of the beauties of motor racing and how it differentiates from so many other sports which have little, if any, reliance on myriad external factors. And we also need to add money to that list. How many drivers have talent wasted for want of a proper budget and sponsor?

In writing this book, I decided that it would be wrong to concentrate purely on Formula 1 drivers. Yes, they have deserved their place in the sport's history, especially those who became world champions, but Britain is a country rich in motorsport and she has produced plenty of outstanding drivers and characters who have made an enormous contribution to the sport without becoming a Formula 1

World Champion. Our Immortals come from F1, yes, but also from American single-seater racing, sports car racing and saloon car racing. As I write in 2023, I am aware of a whole new generation, a whole new demographic of fans attracted to Formula 1 thanks to the hugely successful Netflix series, *Drive to Survive*. Those people have been brilliant for business at Silverstone by boosting ticket sales each year and at teams' merchandising shops but their interest is confined to F1. One hopes that some of them will explore the many other categories motor racing has to offer and that their interest will outlast the current F1 grid.

Some of our Immortals were personal heroes and for their inclusion I make no apology. They captured a small boy's interest and helped to nurture it to the point that, after 45 years of watching the sport, I find myself writing about them. It is interesting to see how many of our Immortals had their careers overlap and how their post-competition careers took them into different walks of life, although perhaps predictably many headed to broadcasting.

So many drivers came close to making the cut and are acknowledged in the Honourable mentions chapter and I am sure that if I sat down to write this in 2033 it would be a different dozen. The sport moves so quickly that one can expect new names to have made their considerable mark in the next decade.

Our drivers are profiled in chronological order, based on their date of birth rather than when they started racing, and I hope that you understand why they are included even if you don't agree. This is a very personal choice of drivers, but I believe I have justified my selection, although I am happy for you to take issue with me over any absentees. I also need to address one other point: Immortal. Impossible, of course, and many of the drivers in these pages are no longer with us so how can such a title be worthwhile? Simple: each of our drivers has achieved outstanding results, fame and a reputation that outlives them. For that they have earned motor racing immortality.

Now, should have I included . . . ? No, stick with the 12 you have chosen. Enjoy!

David Addll

June 2023

Team Lotus gave Graham Hill his Formula 1 debut and the second of his two world championship crowns.

1

GRAHAM HILL

Full name	Norman Graham Hill
Birthdate	15 February 1929 (died 29 November 1975)
Place of birth	Hampstead

Graham Hill was regarded as a grafter rather than a naturally gifted driver, but his success behind the wheel said otherwise.

If there was one driver who brought motor racing, in those long-gone pre-internet and social media days, to the man on the street, it was Graham Hill. There was something about him that the public took to, while not gelling in the same way as the differing characters of his peers, like Jim Clark or Jackie Stewart. Graham Hill came from nothing, became a world champion, a team owner, a celebrity and, by 2023, the only man ever to win the so-called Triple Crown of the F1 world championship, Indianapolis 500 and Le Mans 24 Hours. He overcame adversity, worked incredibly hard to promote himself and look after sponsors and his death in a plane crash, along with five passengers,

robbed the sport of a great ambassador.

Stubborn, determined, straightforward, gruff . . . All adjectives that you will find to use for Norman Graham Hill. So were brave, successful and entertaining. They all added up to a character who the public loved and, indeed, hated to see struggle as he did towards the end of his decorated career. Graham Hill was a relative late starter to motor racing, aged 25, and the first race that he saw was the one he was in! He had already tried his hand at the Brands Hatch race school where one could do four laps in a Cooper-JAP for 25 pence a lap. Graham was intoxicated but faced two problems: the first was that he wanted to do more.

The second difficulty was that he was penniless and couldn't afford to go motor racing. Add another adjective to the list: enterprising. Graham decided to offer his services to Brands Hatch as a mechanic with some of his wages going in lieu of drives. He led his first race but finished second, and toured Europe as a riding mechanic for Jaguar C-type racer Dan Margulies before fate intervened. He found himself at Brands Hatch spectating, but with no means to get home. He started chatting to a bloke in the paddock and convinced the unwitting good Samaritan to give him a lift. That man was Lotus founder Colin Chapman and a bond was instantly forged between the pair. Chapman lent Hill bits with which to build a Lotus XI for 1956, winning at Brands, Silverstone, Mallory Park and Aintree and with those results, and a personable attitude, he was offered drives by other owners eager to see their cars at the front of the grid. Chapman wasn't enamoured of this idea and wanted the rapid Hill to win in a Lotus, signing him as a driver for the latter half of 1957.

For 1958, Graham was a grand prix driver, his debut coming at Monaco in a Lotus 12. A broken half shaft caused retirement as a

He started chatting to a bloke in the paddock and convinced the unwitting good Samaritan to give him a lift. That man was Lotus founder Colin Chapman . . .

wheel parted company with the car, but by the end of Graham's career he would be synonymous with the principality. He would win there five times which made his final appearance in a grand prix weekend, at Monaco in 1975, all the harder to witness. He failed to qualify . . .

After a handful of races with the Lotus 12, Hill drove a Lotus 16 for the second part of the season, the unreliable car failing to showcase his ability. Life was just as frustrating in 1959 as a string of mechanical failures meant that he finished just twice. It made him look elsewhere and so for 1960 he moved to BRM starting a seven-year association. On paper, the season wasn't much better than his time at Lotus, but he did at least take a maiden podium at Zandvoort in the Dutch Grand Prix and led the British GP at Silverstone until he spun off. He walked back

Hill had a sense of humour alright! Here he drives a replica of Henry Ford's first vehicle, the quadricycle. The original quadricycle was built in 1896, constructed of wood and metal and weighed only 500lbs, had a top speed of 20 mph and no brakes!

to the pits to a standing ovation from the fans in the grandstands who had taken the underdog into their hearts. The public affection would grow as his successes came, but they were still some way off with 1961 being another frustrating season as fuel pump gremlins, an oil leak, a crash and two engine failures contributed to a season of numerous non-finishes. For 1961, he needed to take a step forward.

Aboard the BRM P57, Graham Hill entered the 1962 Formula 1 World Championship with only one podium finish to his name. He ended the season as world champion with four wins and he could have taken two more but mechanical woes took him out of two further races that he was leading. The victories came in Holland, Germany, Italy and South Africa, the last being crucial as it gave him the title in the final race of the season, after Christmas on 29 December. Hill and Jim Clark entered the season arguing over the title, but when Clark's Lotus 25 retired with an oil leak, Hill was a worthy champion. In addition, he was winning in the many non-championship Formula 1 races that were regularly on the calendar. He triumphed at Goodwood in the race in which Stirling Moss had his F1 career-ending crash and won a photo-finish in the *Daily Express* International Trophy at Silverstone, starting on pole and just getting the nod over Clark as they flashed past the chequered flag.

Graham Hill won five of his 14 grands prix victories at Monaco.

The following season was a tougher one as Hill was once again pitted against Clark, his Lotus 25 a more reliable car as Hill's BRM suffered a number of mechanical issues, plus he was excluded from third at Reims in the French Grand Prix after he was given a push start and then dropped to third at Silverstone when he ran low on fuel. Even so, he ended the year second in the championship tied on points with Richie Ginther. He was runner-up again in 1964 after two wins kept him in the title race going into the final race in Mexico City. Hill was pitted against Clark and Ferrari's John Surtees, who had already won titles on two wheels and was now mastering four. All Graham had to do was finish third, and that is where he was running in the early stages of the race until the second Ferrari of Lorenzo Bandini made a desperate move for position. Contact was made and Hill was fired off the road into the barriers, the impact damaging his exhaust and necessitating a pit stop. He rejoined to finish 11th, two laps down, as Clark retired and Bandini obeyed team orders to allow Surtees past to win the championship. 'Bandini certainly earned his money that day,' wrote a sanguine Hill at the time, 'apart from the rather desperate effort at the hairpin. A lot of people suggested at the time that it was deliberate but I don't think so. It was obvious to me that he was making a desperate manoeuvre and he just overcooked it.' Such a way of looking at an incident seems alien in the current world where someone must always be at fault.

There was Monaco mastery again in 1965 as he won on the streets on his way, again, to second in the championship, but frustrations were coming as more non-finishes were posted by BRM. In 1966, though, Hill scored one of his best wins and it came in America. In the 50th running of the Indianapolis 500, Hill made his Indy debut having been told by experts that rookies didn't win on their first attempt. They were wrong: fellow first-timer Jackie Stewart led before his Lola T90-Ford retired after a broken scavenge pump caused the fuel pressure to drop and Hill inherited the lead in his Lola. He led only 10 laps but took the chequered flag first, drinking the famous glass of milk in Victory Lane. Later, Clark's team disputed the result believing that, although the Scotsman had spun twice, he was the winner. No way, reckoned Hill: 'I drank the milk.'

For 1967, he surprised people by moving to Lotus as teammate to Jim Clark. While some drivers may have run a mile rather than be pitted against one of the best, Hill relished the opportunity. He was sixth in the championship that winless year but in 1968 he would come into his own as he

Graham Hill explains his art to a royal audience including the future King Charles III.

After the ignominy
of failing to qualify at
Monaco in 1975, Hill came
to the conclusion that his
time was up and he stood
down to run the team.

became team leader after Clark was killed in a Formula 2 accident at Hockenheim in April. Hill won the next two races on the bounce, lifting the spirits of Team Lotus, the squad also losing Mike Spence who had taken over Clark's Indianapolis 500 entry but was killed during practice. Three grand prix wins helped him to take a second world title as he established himself at Colin Chapman's team.

In 1969, he finished second in South Africa at the start of the season and took a fifth victory in Monaco suggesting a third title could be his. Lotus' reliability issues hampered that dream, but the season ended badly in America when he spun at Watkins Glen. As he jumped from the car to push it downhill to restart, he noticed the tyres were past their best and, as he passed the pits, signalled that he would be in next time. Instead, the right rear tyre gave way and pitched the Lotus into a spin, the car hitting

an earth bank and overturning. Hill hadn't done up his seatbelts and was hurled from the cockpit, suffering a fractured right knee, a dislocated left knee and torn ligaments. Many expected this to be the moment Hill announced his retirement but that gritty determination wasn't far from the surface and instead he took a drive for Rob Walker's private Lotus team. His career was in decline, however, and although he won the non-championship BRDC International Trophy at Silverstone in 1971 and the Le Mans 24 Hours for Matra in 1972, he seemed to be out of a drive as, aged 43, he was dropped by Brabham at the end of 1972.

That stubbornness shone through again as Hill instead elected to run his own team and race the cars as well. With backing from Embassy cigarettes through parent company Imperial Tobacco, he drove the new Shadow DN1 without distinction in 1973, forsaking the car for a Lola chassis the following year. After the ignominy of failing to qualify at Monaco in 1975, Hill came to the conclusion that his time was up and he stood down to run the team. Sponsorship was still coming from Embassy and Hill was still in demand, having

Graham Hill was a double world champion as well as winning the Le Mans 24 Hours and the Indianapolis 500, the only driver to win the so-called Triple Crown.

worked hard for sponsors for nearly a decade. Long before his retirement he had used his Indy 500 winnings to buy a Piper Aztec aircraft and flew here and there to conduct testing for teams but also to open supermarkets or other personal appearances. Nothing, it seemed, was too much trouble.

There was more to him than just a grand prix driver. Before he turned his attention to cars he had been a keen member of the London Rowing Club whose colours adorned his crash helmet and had worked as an apprentice engineer at Smiths Industries before being conscripted into the Royal Navy where he served

as an Engine Room Artificer on the HMS *Swiftsure* and rose to the rank of petty officer. He rejoined Smiths after he left the Navy.

As a driver, he seemed to be irrepressible. In addition to his Formula 1 drives in world championship and non-championship races, he won the Sports 1600 class of the 1960 Targa Florio for Porsche, sharing the pretty 718 with Edgar Barth. They were fifth overall in the race that lasted over seven hours with each lap of the Sicilian road course 45 miles long. In 1961, he made history when he won the first race for the stunning Jaguar E-type at Oulton

Park in Cheshire plus he won the Tourist Trophy in 1963 and 1964 at Goodwood in a Ferrari 250GTO as well as the Reims 12 Hours in '64 when he shared a Ferrari 250LM with Jo Bonnier. That win came ahead of the similar car of John Surtees/Lorenzo Bandini who

would play such a big part in the outcome of that year's F1 crown.

Hill raced at Le Mans in 1966, sharing an Alan Mann Racing-run Ford GT40 with Australian Brian Muir, but the car retired with front suspension failure after eight hours and he didn't return to la

Hill assumed the role of Lotus team leader after the death of Jim Clark and guided the squad to more success.

Sarthe until 1972 when he shared a Matra MS670 with Frenchman Henri Pescarolo. In a wet race, their Simca-engined car didn't miss a beat and won by 11 laps, although Graham's joy at the win was tempered by the death of Jo Bonnier, a former teammate and friend who perished after a violent accident on the Sunday morning.

If the public took to Graham Hill, so did the media. He was a regular guest on television chat shows, appeared on 16 episodes of the panel show *Call My Bluff* and presented a series for Thames Television entitled *Advanced Driving with Graham Hill* which ran for six episodes in 1974. He was awarded an OBE, voted to second place in the *BBC Sportsview Personality of the Year* and appeared in John Frankenheimer's excellent movie *Grand Prix* as fictitious driver Bob Turner. He also appeared in *Caravan to Vaccarès*, based on Alistair MacLean's novel, as a helicopter pilot. There was also a reference to him in a Monty Python sketch, proof that he was a mainstream figure. That, though, was at odds with the man himself. His widow, Bette, told journalist David Tremayne that, 'He was an incredibly shy man.

He made himself the clown, but I sat next to him at dinners where he was giving the speech and he was so nervous beforehand.'

If Hill lacked the genius of a Clark or a Moss, for example, he made up for it by hard work and determination. He wasn't a man to take no for an answer or to give up on a task. He admitted to scaring himself on his Spa debut in 1958 and pitted. He had a good talk to himself and went out again to qualify 15th of the 20-strong entry. It was the unwillingness to give in that elongated his career, some believing that it went on too long, that the British hero was in danger of becoming a sad figure as the results no longer came and the plum drives petered out. The Le Mans win bucked that trend, but there was almost relief when he called time on his career. The commitment was there to be channelled into operating his team and to promoting the career of his star driver Tony Brise.

In November 1975, the team had been testing its Hill GH2 chassis at Paul Ricard in the South of France and Graham elected to fly home at the end of the final day. With him were Brise, team manager Ray Brimble, designer Andy Smallman and mechanics Tony Alcock and Terry Richards, and Hill flew them home in his Piper PA-23 Aztec twin-engined plane with the weather over the UK deteriorating rapidly. Heading for Elstree Airfield, the Piper became enveloped in thick fog and clipped the treetops over the Arkley golf course causing it to crash. Radio and television programmes were interrupted with the news as no-one was prepared for such a tragedy. Having survived 176 grands prix, to die in such a way seemed a ridiculous waste. Everyone on board was killed and subsequently Hill was found to have transgressed many aviation regulations. The plane, registered initially in the USA, had been removed from the Federal Aviation Administration register and was 'unregistered and stateless' despite still carrying all its original markings. Hill's American FAA pilot certification had expired as had his instrument rating and his UK Instrument Meteorological Conditions rating that would have allowed him to fly in the weather conditions that night, was also out of date and thus invalid. It meant Hill was uninsured and the resulting litigation brought by the administrators of Smallman's estate against Hill's widow, Bette, wiped

out much of Hill's wealth in settling the case. An investigation proved that Hill wasn't intoxicated, that the plane was well-maintained and that Hill himself was an experienced pilot. The exact cause of the accident could not be determined.

It was the end of the Hill team, with its core gone, and the cavalier attitude to aviation rules undoubtedly tarnished some of Graham's legacy, but his career outweighed that. To win a world championship, Le Mans and the Indianapolis 500 is a record unmatched by anyone else, Fernando Alonso being the most recent driver to attempt it but coming up short in America. He was charismatic out of the car, erudite, witty and popular and a dogged and determined competitor in it. His versatility, in single-seaters and sports cars, was added to by occasional outings in the British Saloon Car Championship in a Jaguar Mk2 and Lotus Cortina – he won in both, of course – and even rallying as he tackled the Monte Carlo Rally in 1959 in a Ford Zephyr, in 1960 with a Ford Anglia, a Sunbeam Rapier in 1962 (he finished 10th) and aFord Falcon Sprint in 1964. He also took motoring journalist

Hill won the Indianapolis 500 in 1966, brought into the Mecom Racing Team after the death of driver Walt Hangsen. Hill's appointment came so late that he wasn't even in the entry list in the official programme for the event.

Maxwell Boyd with him on the 1966 RAC International Rally of Great Britain in an Austin Mini Cooper S until the diff failed.

Hill loved driving, no matter what it was. For someone who discovered the sport late he crammed many miles into his career and the name lived on. Son Damon rallied the Williams team after the death of Ayrton Senna in 1994, much as Graham had needed to do at Lotus, and won the 1996 Formula 1 World Championship,

making the Hill family the first to have two generations of world champion, with Graham's grandson Josh also competing in the sport for a short time.

He would have made a superb ambassador of the sport with a charm and wit that made him ideal to counter the machinations of the increasingly commercialised sport. Undoubtedly his was a life taken too soon, but an unrivalled CV makes Graham Hill one of the greatest ever British racing drivers.

Sir Stirling Moss OBE remained a popular – and dashing – motor racing figure at historic racing celebrations until well into his eighties.

2

STIRLING MOSS

Full name	Stirling Craufurd Moss
Birthdate	17 September 1929 (died 12 April 2020)
Place of birth	West Kensington

For many, Stirling Moss was the greatest racing driver
ever and remained in the public eye until his death.

To many, Stirling Moss was the greatest driver never to win the world championship. To others, he was simply the greatest driver of all, victorious as he was in anything to which he turned his hand. In the late 1950s, he was given the sobriquet of Mr Motor Racing by Fleet Street and the name stuck, largely because for most of his 15-year frontline career, he was the most significant man in British motorsport: grands prix, sports cars, rallies . . . Stirling Craufurd Moss could turn his hand to anything.

It was while Moss was at the height of his powers that his career-affecting accident happened. Easter Monday 1962 was the day Stirling headed to Goodwood to drive in the non-championship Formula 1 race for the Glover Trophy. That

season, Moss was due to drive the unthinkable: a privateer Ferrari. Such was his ability that Enzo Ferrari was desperate to have him in one of his cars, but the patriotic Moss refused to leave his friend Rob Walker and his team. A deal was struck, to the amazement of many, for Moss to drive a privateer Ferrari for Walker's team. As it was being readied, Stirling drove a Lotus 18/21 at Goodwood, but, after a pit stop, he was two laps down and, with a win out of the question, set off to break the lap record. Heading into St Mary's corner at over 100 mph, Moss inexplicably went off the road and slammed into the earth bank. His injuries included severe concussion and any memory of the accident and its cause were lost. Indeed, Moss was

'It probably saved his life. He was going faster and faster, taking more risks, and if it hadn't been that accident, it would have been a more serious one.'

unconscious for 38 days and in the list of injuries was a huge trauma to his skull from which his brain had been partly detached meaning that when he regained consciousness, he was unable to speak and was partly paralysed. Moss the fighter went into recovery mode and three months after his accident he left hospital on crutches after having taken all the nurses who had looked after him out for dinner.

The media followed his progress daily, with headlines screaming: 'Stirling Moss in Miracle Escape' (*The Express*), 'Moss: "Life not in danger" – father' (*Evening Standard*) or 'Stirling Moss's crash baffles experts' and the helpful 'What went wrong?' also both from the *Evening Standard*. Once he was out of hospital, the media turned its curiosity to his return to racing, and 14 months after his accident Moss returned to Goodwood to test himself aboard a Lotus 19. The lap times were good but the mental

effort required was too much. 'I have retired,' he announced as he climbed from the car.

In truth, he had retired too early. A year, certainly two, later and his faculties were much improved. Whether he would have been quite as good will never be known, but he would certainly have been competitive and in demand, but the decision had been made and he stuck by it, at least as far as top-line racing was concerned. There would be motor racing again, and for the rest of his 90 years he was a famous racing driver, never forgotten.

The accident stopped his career, but in the opinion of his contemporary Tony Brooks, 'It probably saved his life. He was going faster and faster, taking more risks, and if it hadn't been that accident, it would have been a more serious one.' Moss wanted to win, certainly, and in that desire, he would take risks. Not for Stirling the satisfaction of finishing fifth and banking points. He wanted to win or retire while out front.

Stirling Moss was born into a motor racing family. His father Alfred Moss, whose Jewish father had changed the family surname from Moses, raced at Brookland and even finished 16th at Indianapolis

Stirling Moss remained a household name decades after his retirement from the top of the sport.

Perhaps Stirling's greatest win of all came in the 1955 Mille Miglia in which he and Denis Jenkinson blasted their Mercedes-Benz 300 SLR to victory on the public road course by just under 32 minutes.

in 1924, while his mother Aileen competed in trials and rallies. Following in his mother's footsteps, Stirling first competed on horseback, winning plenty of trophies before switching to cars and taking to hillclimbing in 1948 at Prescott and Shelsley Walsh where he learned the art of a fast getaway. For his entire career Moss was a rapid starter and that first season netted 10 wins out of 14 races once he switched to the circuits. He headed abroad in 1949 racing his Cooper 500 in Italy, aware that to become a professional racing driver he needed to go where the start money was and that first £50 was one of the many deals Moss cut during his career. Next was a sports car ride as, although Jaguar didn't operate a works team, it did sell its XK120 models to selected owners, but the company was concerned when Tommy Wisdom offered young Moss a drive in his car for the Tourist Trophy to be run at Dundrod, one of the most challenging circuits. That it was then run in torrential rain was a concern, but Moss

Five national event wins came, he finished third in the Belgian Grand Prix and led the Italian Grand Prix before the oil tank split and he retired.

demolished the opposition and won the race convincingly, the day before he turned 21. He won £1400 as well.

In 1951, Moss became even busier, a drive here and a drive there. In 13 weeks, he drove in 25 races, many for HWM and he took 19 wins that season. In 1952, though, Moss suffered a frustrating season, second place in the Monte Carlo Rally notwithstanding. Just pause there for a moment: imagine a current Formula 1 driver finding the time, inclination or permission to tackle a major rally during a racing season. After the Monte, Moss was slated to drive the ERA G-type, as he was always a driver who wanted to be in a British car, but when he eventually drove it, was far from impressed. 'It was, above all, a project which made an awful lot of fuss about doing very little. I would eventually learn that even the most brilliant concept could fail if the team concerned lacks the manpower and

organisation and money to develop the inevitable bugs out of it.'

In 1953 Moss drove the new Cooper-Alta but was hampered again by reliability dramas, such as a disintegrating flywheel at Reims which caused shrapnel to gash his leg and that prompted his father to consider his son's future. Word on the grapevine was that Mercedes-Benz was planning a return to racing in 1954 and so Alfred Moss, along with Stirling's manager Ken Gregory, went to see the imposing team manager Alfred Neubauer to ask if Stirling could have a drive. Neubauer said no, impressing upon them the need for Moss to achieve results first, and suggested they abandon jingoism and buy a Maserati 250F. It was a pivotal decision in the career of Stirling Moss.

Five national event wins came, he finished third in the Belgian Grand Prix and led the Italian Grand Prix before the oil tank split and he retired. When Neubauer offered his condolences, it was clear he had been watching the young Brit all season and for 1955 Moss was a factory Mercedes-Benz driver, taking in grands prix and major sports car races.

Moss with his parents, Aileen and Alfred.

That season, Mercedes entered Moss in the Mille Miglia, a terrifying race around 1000 miles of Italian public roads. Motorsport was a different animal back then . . . Moss gave the event his professional all, not going there just to make up the numbers. He reasoned that if he had a navigator alongside, as the rules allowed, telling him what to expect around the next corner, he would be able to commit more and hence go faster. Journalist

Denis Jenkinson was to be Moss's wingman and the pair spent time driving the route and making notes. It meant that when the race started, Moss could keep his foot to the floor because Jenkinson's instructions confirmed that he could and the two dominated the event in a manner never seen before: on roads they barely knew they won by a little under 32 minutes. It remains one of the sport's finest performances.

Later that season, Moss won his first Formula 1 World Championship race, the British Grand Prix held at Aintree. Stirling headed home his teammate Juan Manuel Fangio and while some asked if Fangio had allowed Moss to win, Moss had looked in control all race. He won the Tourist Trophy again that year, once more for Mercedes, but after one of the German cars, driven by Pierre Levegh, had cartwheeled into the Le Mans crowd, killing 81 people, Mercedes withdrew from the sport at the season's end. That meant Moss would be back aboard a Maserati for 1956 with Fangio heading the rival Ferrari assault. Stirling opened his account with the Italian firm with wins in Monaco and Italy, but for the non-championship International Trophy, Maserati would be absent, and Moss needed a car. Vanwall offered him a seat and here was everything that Stirling seemed to want: a well-run British car capable of winning races. He signed for Tony Vandervell's team for 1957 but the season didn't start in the fairy-tale way, as at Monaco he crashed at the chicane and then while waterskiing on holiday, a plume of water went up his nose and he contracted a sinus infection. He bounced back to qualify on pole position for the British Grand Prix

A home win came in the 1955 British Grand Prix at Aintree in which Moss defeated the similar Mercedes W196 of teammate Juan Manuel Fangio by two-tenths of a second.

Moss was a patriotic man and driving a British car appealed to him. In the Vanwall, he took three grand prix wins in 1958.

and he dashed off into the lead only for his car to develop a misfire after 22 laps. The sister car of Tony Brooks was called into the pits and, with Brooks not fully recovered from a Le Mans crash, Moss took over and the pair shared the winning car as Formula 1 rules then allowed.

Come 1958 and Moss was the master on the grid, yet to win the world championship but after the retirement of Fangio was the man to beat. He won four grands prix that season and headed to Casablanca for the final race in with a shout of the championship, but his main opposition was Mike

Hawthorn who had won but one *grande épreuve* that year. To be world champion, Moss needed to win and set fastest lap with Hawthorn third or lower. One reason that they were so close on points was that Moss had helped Hawthorn secure second place in Portugal, where Stirling had won. After Hawthorn had spun on the street circuit's last lap, he headed against the traffic flow to turn around and officials disqualified him. Moss pointed out that Hawthorn wasn't on the track but on the footpath and officials reinstated Mike in the results. Hence, he was in with a title shot.

And so in Casablanca Moss won, set fastest lap and Hawthorn was . . . second. He was the world champion and Moss missed out again, by just one point.

Rule changes looming for 1961 triggered Vandervell to withdraw from the sport and hence Moss was forced to find an alternative team for 1959. Rob Walker's team was the choice as Moss again wanted to drive a British car and Rob ran a Cooper, but the car often suffered with transmission dramas in its Colotti gearbox which, oddly, Moss was causing. He was changing gear early to save the box but it transpired later that had he changed gear at higher revs he would have done less damage, so rather than saving the engine, he paid the price for a gentle approach. Another change came a year later, off to Lotus next but he suffered a major accident at Spa-Francorchamps when a wheel came adrift and Moss left the road suffering a broken nose, crushed vertebrae and broken legs. He returned late in the season, but it was another year in which the championship eluded him.

He stayed with a Lotus, run by Rob Walker, for 1961 and won in Monaco (one of his greatest drives

Moss drove a massive variety of cars in his career, not just in Formula 1, but in touring cars, sports cars, rallies and even record attempts.

to fend off a trio of Ferraris for 100 laps) and Germany and that prompted Enzo Ferrari to make that extraordinary exception for him of a privateer car for 1962. And then came *that* accident.

Moss drove a massive variety of cars in his career, not just in Formula 1, but in touring cars, sports cars, rallies and even record attempts.

In truth, while he never returned to top-level racing, the retirement wasn't as long as some believe. For example, in 1968, just six years after the Goodwood accident, he drove in the 84-hour, yes . . . 84, *Marathon de la Route* at the Nürburgring with Innes Ireland and Claudio Maglioli and they were leading their class when their Lancia Fulvia's gearbox broke. In 1974 he drove a Mercedes 280E in the World Cup Rally, but its gearbox broke in the middle of the Sahara Desert. Then, in 1976, he was tempted to race in

'I realised that if I drove fast enough to beat the people I thought I ought to beat, I would no longer be enjoying myself.'

Australia, partnering Jack Brabham in a Holden Torana in the Bathurst 1000 touring car classic. Brabham stalled on the grid and was hit from behind, but the damaged car returned to the race for Moss to drive before it dropped a valve. In 1979, he drove a Volkswagen Golf with Denny Hulme in New Zealand and that prompted a decision to sign for Audi for 1980 to drive in the British Saloon Car Championship, now the BTCC, in an Audi 80. It wasn't an experience Moss enjoyed, as for one thing he had never raced on slick tyres before and found them unenjoyable, while the rather robust way that saloon car drivers raced was alien to someone whose talents were forged in a different era, on unforgiving circuits. But he wasn't done with racing . . .

Historic racing in the UK was blossoming and he was tempted back to drive a Maserati 250F, Aston Martin DBR1, Maserati T61, the list went on. He was successful too and owners wanted him to drive for them, while event promoters were happy to have him on the entry list. On each appearance that Moss was competing he was trying, pushing. Never was he there just for a fee, just to make up the numbers, just to keep his name known. Yes, he was a brand and publicity helped, but he was as competitive in historic races as he had been in his heyday. And it was that competitive spirit, his desire to be racing not just driving, that motivated him and it was that need to remain competitive that prompted the ultimate decision. At Le Mans in 2011, Moss was competing in the historic event supporting the 24-hour race and at the end of qualifying he climbed from his Porsche RS61, a competitive time established, and said: 'That's it. Going down the Mulsanne Straight just now, I realised that if I drove fast enough to beat the people I thought I ought to beat, I would no longer be enjoying myself.' And that was it: with no sentimentality but complete practicality, aged 81 years and nine months, Stirling Moss finally retired.

After his Goodwood accident and decision to stop racing he

Moss triumphed in his Lotus 18-Climax in the 1961 Monaco Grand Prix, 100 gruelling laps being a test for man and machine.

was in demand for media and PR work. He turned his hand to commentary for ABC in America and late in life found fame for a whole new generation by narrating the children's TV series *Roary the Racing Car*. Sponsors queued up to use him, such as BP which accounts for why he even appeared behind the wheel of an Austin A60 in a Banger race at Wimbledon Stadium, backed by the oil company. He had a property company and various other business involvements, ran his own racing team (SMART: Stirling Moss Automobile Racing Team), was an ambassador for car manufacturers, petrol companies and banks. He was in demand

Moss celebrates at Silverstone after winning the 1961 British Empire Trophy in Rob Walker's Cooper T53-Climax.

as an after-dinner speaker and after recovering from prostate cancer endorsed a medication for erectile dysfunction. There was a cameo role for him in the original *Casino Royale* movie, he played himself in *The Beauty Jungle* and for many years, the question 'Who do you think you are? Stirling Moss?' was posed by British policemen to speeding drivers.

Mind you, there were occasional dissenters to the Moss marketing, such as cartoonist Willie Rushton who produced a page in *Private Eye* magazine mocking Stirling. Rushton's character was called Rolling Stone (gathers no . . . OK, you got it) and pointedly

noted that he introduced 'TV programmes on subjects about which he knows nothing.' Ouch. Moss, mind you, rang the *Eye* to ask if he could use it as a Christmas card. Indeed, Stirling was happy to make jokes at his own expense, such as walking down a street to dinner when a gaggle of people came towards him. 'Look,' exclaimed one, 'It's Stirling Moss!' to which Stirling swung around and shouted: 'Where? Where?'

The many engagements were co-ordinated by his third wife, Lady Susie, who he had met in the 1950s as he knew her family. They got together in 1977 and were married in 1980 and she was his constant companion, his aide, his soulmate. Their 40th anniversary would have been five days after he died and Lady Susie Moss died in March 2023.

Moss stayed in touch with modern motor racing and was a regular visitor to grands prix. He had his views on the salaries that today's drivers commanded and the safety measures in place compared to his day. 'Cornering at the maximum when there's a nice smooth lawn each side is difficult. Doing it when there's a brick wall on one side and a precipice on the other –

that's an achievement.' He hadn't been a professional racing driver since 1962 and yet he remained in demand, and famous, for the rest of his life. Few sports people have been taken into the nation's heart quite like Stirling Moss and he retained that affection to the end.

Stirling Moss could drive anything anywhere. He treated everyone, friends or fans, with equal courtesy just as he did rivals on the track, but that said, he was the hardest competitor out there. 'I don't want to be remembered as a driver. I want to be remembered as a racer,' he once said.

That, unquestionably, he was. Sir Stirling Craufurd Moss OBE was motor racing royalty.

The Ferguson P99 is the only four-wheel drive car to win a Formula 1 race. Stirling Moss heads for victory in the non-championship Oulton Park Gold Cup in 1961.

A world champion on two and four wheels makes John Surtees unique

3

JOHN SURTEES

Full name	John Norman Surtees
Birthdate	11 February 1934 (died 10 March 2017)
Place of birth	Tatsfield

John Surtees won on two and four wheels as well as building his own cars to leave a massive impression on the sport.

John Surtees had already immortalised himself before he first sat in a racing car. An outstanding motorcycle racer, John was seven-times a world champion, first on 350cc machinery and then in 500s, before he changed his focus to car racing. He was a world champion on four wheels as well, the only man in history to achieve such a feat. That he went on to be an entrant and constructor as well as the figurehead of Team GB in the A1GP Cup of Nations series merely added to his legend.

John Norman Surtees was born into a motorcycling family. His father, Jack, was an accomplished amateur bike racer and John started his career in 1951, having passengered for his father in grasstrack sidecar races. He started as an apprentice at Vincent Motorcycles and, aboard a Grey Flash, won his first race at Brands Hatch and became synonymous with Nortons in his early days before he moved to MV Agustas. Success in the 500cc world championship came first, in 1956, a title he won again in 1958, 1959 and 1960. If that weren't enough, John doubled up with 350cc world titles in 1958, 1959 and 1960 making him the outstanding rider of the day. His desire to go racing meant that he wanted to compete in the Isle of Man TT, where he became the first man to win the Senior TT three years in a row, as well as in national events which irked team owner Count Domenico Agusta who was reluctant to let his prized rider risk himself outside the world championship. So, Surtees looked at car racing and a new career was born.

The four-wheeled story began in 1960 at Goodwood aboard a Cooper Formula Junior chassis run by Ken Tyrrell. Surtees was second to Jim Clark and instantly the paddock was buzzing about his ability. Colin Chapman was the first on the phone and offered Surtees a drive in a Lotus 18 and John was blisteringly fast, finishing second to Jack

John Surtees first displayed his bravery on two wheels where world championships came on 350cc and 500cc machines.

Brabham in just his second grand prix and he led his third in Portugal before a broken radiator heralded his demise. Although he drove in just four grands prix, and finished only one, he had done enough to entice a contract from Chapman for 1961, but Surtees was less than impressed by Colin's attitude to his drivers. Instead, he elected to sign for the Yeoman Credit-sponsored team running Coopers, but the team achieved modest results, save for a win in Goodwood's Glover Trophy. A year later the Coopers were replaced by Lolas and Surtees became more involved in developing the cars which certainly helped, but although he bagged a couple of second places, he was still frustrated in his quest to win a grand prix. For 1963, that would change, and it would do so by putting the Englishman back in an Italian environment, such as in his successful motorcycling days: he signed for Ferrari.

It was a gamble because the team seemed to have lost its way but Surtees was able to galvanise the team as a driver and with technical input. Such was the Englishman's standing that this was the second time he had been approached by Enzo Ferrari: the first offer had

It was a gamble because the team seemed to have lost its way but Surtees was able to galvanise the team as a driver and with technical input.

been rebuffed for 1962, but Ferrari held Surtees in such regard that he tried again. Few drivers can lay claim to such an accolade. He won in Germany that season, finally scoring that elusive maiden GP success, but it was a long wait for the second as Ferrari, with Surtees, developed the monocoque 156 chassis. In 1964, Surtees was armed with the new 158 model with a V8 engine and this, finally, completed the package that he craved. He won again in Germany and then in Italy which naturally made him a star in the eyes of *Il Commendatore* not to mention an entire nation. Not only that but Surtees headed to Mexico with a chance of winning the world championship that season against Graham Hill and Jim Clark. When Clark's engine suffered an oil leak and Hill tangled with the second Ferrari of Lorenzo Bandini, Surtees crossed the line second which was enough to win him the world championship and complete a staggering achievement: a world champion on two and four wheels and to be F1 world champion in just five seasons.

If 1964 gave Surtees the highs of motor racing, the following year was to offer the lows. Having come from motorcycle racing, often regarded as the more dangerous branch of motorsport, it was perhaps ironic that it was on four wheels that Surtees suffered his biggest injuries while driving in Canada. In days gone by, long before such rigid commercial constraints and tight contracts of today, drivers could race almost anything, anywhere, anytime. So it was that Ferrari driver John Surtees ran his own team, Team Surtees, in the Can-Am sports car series, in, as the name suggests, America and Canada. Aboard his Lola T70, John suffered a massive accident at Mosport Park when a hub carrier failed and the car

cleared a barrier. Soaked in fuel and trapped under the wreckage, he suffered injuries to his back, legs and hip and local hospital medic Dr McGoey explained that he was lucky not to have suffered paralysis. In reality, John was lucky to be alive. McGoey described his patient as a 'Stiff-upper-lip Englishman who is determined to make a rapid recovery.' Surtees certainly did that, focusing on a return to racing and to Ferrari.

His 1965 F1 season had been a challenge as well, but Enzo Ferrari kept faith in the Englishman and once John was out of London's St Thomas's Hospital in January 1966, he set about returning to fitness. Ferrari may have kept faith, but not so the headline-hungry Italian media who were quick to put out the story that Surtees wouldn't be strong enough to cope with the new breed of heavier three-litre Formula 1 cars. Surtees, never a quitter, went to Modena to test a car over a full race distance and in so doing broke the lap record. He won the non-championship Syracuse Grand Prix and also took the Monza 1000 kilometre sports car race, sharing his Ferrari with Mike Parkes. Thus, he headed to the opening

> In days gone by, long before such rigid commercial constraints and tight contracts of today, drivers could race almost anything, anywhere, anytime.

John Surtees rode in 15 races in the Isle of Man TT and won six of them.

GP at Monaco in late May more confident and proceeded to lead the race until his engine failed, but he was unstoppable in the Belgian rain at Spa-Francorchamps next time out to the delight of Ferrari. Not, though, to the delight of everyone as internally there was a Machiavellian subplot taking shape led by team manager Eugenio Dragoni. He favoured the team's number two driver Lorenzo Bandini and was actively playing one off against the other and it all came to a head at Le Mans where Surtees was due to share a Ferrari 330 P3 with Mike Parkes, but when Dragoni learned that new Fiat chairman Gianni Agnelli would be attending, Dragoni switched Surtees to a different car and put Agnelli's nephew, Ludovico Scarfiotti, in with Parkes. Surtees was livid and walked out of Ferrari there and then. A fit of pique maybe, but Surtees was single-minded enough to know what he wanted and to demand it. It would be a lifelong trait that, on occasions, had a detrimental effect. Even as soon as 1967 Ferrari realised that things needed changing and fired Dragoni. It was too late for Surtees, though. Years later, Surtees and Ferrari both agreed that his departure hurt both parties.

He would later admit that: 'I was impetuous. I was younger and more aggressive. Looking back now, I could have reasoned it through more carefully. That said, I still felt, then and now, like a part of the Ferrari family. I didn't agree with everything that went on, but you don't in families, do you?'

His Ferrari career over, midway through the 1966 world championship Surtees found a home at Cooper and raised two

John Surtees only won six grands prix, but it was with Ferrari that he put together his most consistent season to win the 1964 world championship.

metaphorical fingers to Dragoni and Ferrari by winning in Mexico at the end of the season and the fact that he finished runner-up in the world championship to Jack Brabham, thereby beating the Ferrari drivers, underlined Dragoni's mistake in alienating Surtees.

Never one to shirk a challenge, Surtees agreed to drive for Honda in 1967 as the Japanese giant made a return to grand prix racing and John liked the thought of helping to turn the cars into winners. It was a challenge alright, with Surtees being frustrated by the demands of working with a large organisation and progress was slow as the Honda RA273 with its V12 engine was heavy and temperamental. Eventually, he could accept the situation no longer and elected to miss the Canadian Grand Prix, but he didn't walk away: instead, he headed to his old mates at Lola and, in five weeks, they built the Honda RA300 which he debuted at the Italian Grand Prix. The *tifosi* still loved *Il Grande John* and he them, so after a last-corner battle with Jack Brabham he was a popular winner in a truly remarkable turnaround of fortunes. Sadly, that would be his last grand prix win as he stayed with Honda for 1968 and the car proved to

be unreliable as gearboxes failed, alternators lost drive, rear wings fell off, engines overheated and batteries went flat. He took pole in Italy, cue more cheers from the crowd, but crashed avoiding an errant Chris Amon. Seventh in the championship, it was time to move on. On top of helping the team and designing a car, he was also involved in negotiating contracts, travel arrangements and sorting race entries. He was more than a driver and while that involvement may have been seen as a commitment to the project, it was a frustration to those who felt undermined. It was a situation that would affect his own team in later years.

BRM was a team with a proud record but, by 1969, was being run by the eccentric and autocratic Louis Stanley. Having married into the Owen family which owned BRM, Stanley was never short of self-belief and was not overly interested in alternative opinions. Surtees was similar in some ways and so the marriage of the parties for 1969 was watched with interest. It wasn't a successful season, as Surtees finished 11th, without a win. Stanley wrote of Surtees: 'I found him a pain in the neck. That he meant well is perhaps the kindest comment. If theoretical planning could win a race, Surtees would have taken many chequered flags but somehow it rarely happened.'

Surtees, naturally, heaped the blame on the team: 'Without a doubt my worst year of racing. I'd rather not discuss it, frankly. That was just paying penance. It was hell. At the end of that year my health, physical and mental, was at a very low level. I considered getting out of motor racing altogether.'

Instead, as Stanley pontificated: 'When a driver fancies himself as a technical engineer with the expertise to cope with sophisticated Formula 1 machinery, it is far better for him to stake his opinions in his own set-up.' Surtees did just that and started building his own F1 cars for 1970, having started the season aboard a McLaren. The first Surtees, the TS5, was a Formula 5000 car which was a reworked Leda chassis. The TS type number was for Team Surtees as the JS tag had been applied to motorcycle projects and the TS7 was the first F1 car debuted at the 1970 British Grand Prix. The car was quick but retired with a lack of oil pressure and while John won the non-championship race at Oulton Park, the Gold Cup, fifth in the Canadian

> But a delegator he was not: he designed the cars, drove the cars, ran the team and everything had to be done his way.

Grand Prix was the car's best world championship result. Life was no easier in 1971, when with backing from Brooke Bond Oxo, a fifth place in Holland was the team's best as the new TS9 suffered retirements from a variety of trivial matters.

In 1972, Surtees had to face the realities of life: he couldn't afford to turn away pay drivers and hence drove in just one race as seats were taken by drivers paying to be in the car. He should have raced twice, but failed to start the US GP at Watkins Glen when there was no spare engine for his car . . .

That was it as far as Surtees the driver was concerned. Although he returned to win the 1981 Oulton Park Gold Cup, by now a race for historic cars, his contemporary driving days were done as he concentrated on running Team Surtees. Here, his personality was both help and hindrance as he was a stickler for things done his way and his commitment was without question. But a delegator

In 1966, Surtees fell out with Ferrari and switched to a Maserati-powered Cooper T81. He won in Mexico and finished second in the world championship.

he was not: he designed the cars, drove the cars, ran the team and everything had to be done his way. Occasionally he would admit that he shouldn't be doing everything but he didn't have the budget to employ people to do the job, yet those in the team would confirm that they weren't empowered to undertake even the most basic of tasks. Hovering in the background was someone wanting him to sort out the petty cash or sign a cheque and Surtees in turn complained of his long working hours. He was direct, which didn't always endear him to his staff, nor the press corps

as he would devour every race report and fire off a lengthy letter to the editor if he felt his team had been wronged. Small wonder that as the team declined, so did his reputation. Sympathy for Surtees in the 1970s was in short supply.

His brusque nature didn't help retain staff nor sponsors. Unable to do the job with an insufficient budget, his enthusiasm for the sport waned and in 1978 he closed the team and retreated from motor racing, although it would be wrong to suggest that the Surtees team or cars had been entirely unsuccessful, for in 1972

Mike Hailwood took the European Formula 2 Championship crown aboard a Surtees TS10. Fittingly, Hailwood had previously been a star on two wheels and mirrored Surtees's career when 'Mike the Bike' switched to car racing.

Once he had walked away from motor racing, Surtees turned his attentions to business where he ran a motorcycle shop in West Wickham in Kent and had a Honda dealership in Edenbridge as well as being a regular in classic motorcycle events. He succeeded in property development and seemed to have faded away from motor racing until the A1GP series was created in 2005. The category was for single-seater cars that raced for a country rather than a team, and so Team Great Britain took on teams from around the globe. He was the chairman of Team Great Britain and threw himself into the role during the category's brief history before financial problems forced its demise. His interest in the sport was triggered when his son, Henry, from his third wife took up racing and he returned to his roots, taking Henry karting and then into circuit racing. Inspired by the karting scene, Surtees bought the Buckmore Park circuit

in 2015 and it passed into the hands of his daughter, Leonora Martell-Surtees, after his death.

Surtees was awarded an MBE and then an OBE (in 2008) and for many years there was a part of the British media that felt a knighthood should also be afforded to him, but it never came. Instead, in 2016, he became a Commander of the Order of the British Empire (CBE). He was inducted into the International Motorsports Hall of Fame and the FIM, motorcycle racing's governing body, honoured him as a Grand Prix Legend in 2003.

He raced in the most dangerous of eras and in the most dangerous of disciplines, but his Mosport Park accident aside, he passed without many injuries. It was then a ghastly irony that his beloved son, Henry, should die of injuries sustained in an accident at Brands Hatch in 2009, when struck on the head by an errant wheel ripped from a car that had crashed ahead of him. Surtees coped as he knew how by throwing himself into founding a charity called the Henry Surtees Foundation, dedicated to assisting victims of accidental brain damage and to promote safety in driving in motorsport. On his death of respiratory failure in 2017, Surtees was buried next to Henry at St Peter and St Paul's Church in Lingfield, Surrey.

Surtees was a fine rider and driver whose accomplishments are often overlooked by the relative failure of his team and by his messy career, affected as it was by his no-nonsense personality. He was a winner not only in Formula 1 but also in sports cars. He was one of the few drivers to turn to team ownership and to race car construction successfully, for while the Team Surtees single-seaters of

Surtees was perfectly suited to the powerful 1960s sports car races. Aboard a Lola T70 Spyder, Surtees retired from this round of the British Sports Car Championship at Silverstone when he lost a wheel.

Surtees was a racer, a winner, a team owner and a constructor who made a massive impact on the sport.

Formula 1 may not have achieved titles, the squad did so in Can-Am and the TS10 was a force in Formula 2. It is tempting, unfairly, to remember the end of his career and the decline of the Formula 1 team rather than his extraordinary efforts at his peak.

Others from two wheels have switched to four, Hailwood and then Giacomo Agostini in the 1970s, and Damon Hill began his career on bikes before moving to cars, but none have emulated the success of Surtees. True, both disciplines are different today from the '50s and '60s when Surtees competed, but that shouldn't decry his efforts. To win any world championship is a tremendous achievement. Seven on two wheels is quite something and then to win a Formula 1 World Championship as well is outstanding.

From 111 GP starts, Surtees won only six races but that is more to mechanical deficiencies than a lack of ability. Nobody has transcended the two different strands of motorsport like John Surtees did and his is a record that is unlikely to be equalled. That certainly earns him a unique legacy.

Surtees began racing on two wheels in 1952 and never lost his love for motorcycle racing.

Jim Clark, the quiet and unassuming Scottish farmer gelled with Colin Chapman's Team Lotus.

4

JIM CLARK

Full name	James Clark, Jr
Birthdate	4 March 1936 (died 7 April 1968)
Place of birth	Kilmany

Jim Clark's death in 1968 shocked the motor racing world. He was so good, said his rivals, that if he could be killed, what chance did they have?

If Jim Clark could be killed in a racing car, then so could anyone. It has become a cliché in motor racing, but it stands true as well. The quiet, unassuming Duns farmer was a sublime talent who made driving, winning, look effortless until his death in a Formula 2 race at Hockenheim in 1968. Racing drivers knew the sport was dangerous, true, but this brought them all up with a jolt. Jimmy? Dead? In a racing car?

There is little period footage of the softly spoken Scotsman, although photographs abound, normally of him in a Lotus as his relationship with Colin Chapman was the perfect one. They had a bond that few team owners and drivers achieve and they racked up success after success. Clark always felt he was a farmer first and a racing driver second, happier on the hills of Chirnside than a grand prix paddock. Despite his successes, motor racing began as a pastime rather than a career and his early life was that of farming until a friendship developed with another local farmer, Ian Scott Watson. Jimmy, who was handy on the local roads, entered a sprint in a Sunbeam Talbot in 1956 at Stobs Camp and won his class, although the opposition wasn't the best. A week later Jim accompanied Scott Watson to the bleak Crimond circuit north of Aberdeen where he was given a chance behind the wheel of Ian's three-cylinder DKW saloon and the aspiring young

Jim Clark scored early success in Formula Junior, winning in his Lotus 18 at Goodwood in March 1960.

racer lapped three seconds faster than the tiny saloon had ever gone. Scott Watson insisted Clark race the German saloon and he finished eighth, cementing the belief that here was a star in the making.

For 1957, Clark tackled a number of sprints but was handed Scott Watson's new Porsche 1600 Super for the end of the season and Jim won a handicap race at Charterhall

and from that a racing career beckoned. There was, however, one problem: most of the star Scottish drivers already raced for David Murray's successful Ecurie Ecosse team which attracted trade support thanks to its Le Mans victories in 1956 and 1957. Scott Watson and fellow local motoring enthusiast Jock McBain decided that they had to take the fight to Ecurie Ecosse

History would show, however, that Spa along with Zandvoort, would give him more grand prix successes than any other venue.

and formed Border Reivers as a rival team, the title from the ancient name for a bunch of marauding Scots. With just five races to his name, Jim Clark found himself on the grid in a Jaguar D-type at Charterhall where he made history by becoming the first sports car driver to lap any post-war British circuit at over 100 mph. He raced next at Spa, a circuit that he came to dislike, partly due to the death of Archie Scott Brown in Clark's first race at the Belgian road circuit. History would show, however, that Spa along with Zandvoort, would give him more grand prix successes than any other venue. By the time of his death, Clark would have won four times in the Ardennes forest.

At the end of 1958, Clark raced his new Border Reivers Lotus Elite at Brands Hatch on Boxing Day where he found himself against Lotus founder Colin Chapman, a win lost only to an errant backmarker. Chapman saw for

himself what Scott Watson had seen: a supremely talented driver and one who should be in a Lotus permanently. Before that could happen, though, Clark was asked to join Ecurie Ecosse for the 1959 Tourist Trophy at Goodwood, where he shared a Tojeiro-Jaguar with American Masten Gregory who had one of his regular accidents and the car retired. Although he had agreed to drive for Aston Martin, its Formula 1 project never got going which enabled him to sign for Chapman for 1960: a Formula Junior and a Formula 2 programme were on the table. It started an extraordinary career in which Clark would drive for no other grand prix team, and his debut in Formula 1 came as early as 1960 when John Surtees, a Lotus F1 driver, had a clashing motorcycle commitment, the Isle of Man TT Races. Different times . . .

Chapman persuaded Clark that he was ready for F1 and hence he made his debut at the Dutch Grand Prix, Jimmy running fourth before his Lotus 18 retired. He was, Chapman said, ready for F1 full-time and his next race would come at Spa, where once again Jimmy would have to face the realities of motor racing at the time. Chris

Bristow had been busy battling with Willy Mairesse when they collided and Bristow was killed, Clark witnessing marshals removing the dead body and discovered post-race of the death of another British driver, Alan Stacey, who was killed when a bird flew into his face. These fatalities, as well as a major accident for Stirling Moss in which he suffered serious injuries, did little to appease Jimmy's feelings for the brooding Belgian circuit.

A first podium finish came at the end of 1960 in just his fifth grand prix, his Lotus 18 taking third in Oporto, and two more followed in 1961. For 1962, Lotus unveiled its beautiful Type 25 chassis, and it was perfectly suited to Clark's effortless and easy style. It had a monocoque body and a Climax V8 engine and although clutch problems halted progress at Zandvoort and Monaco, things changed for round three at Clark's detested Spa. Dramas in qualifying meant he would start on row five after relatively little running before the race. His first flying lap was five seconds faster than his best effort in practice and seven laps in, he set the fastest lap. He moved up to second, chasing teammate Trevor Taylor who was content to wave him by. Once ahead, Clark disappeared to win by 44 seconds, a maiden victory taken, a significant defeat of his Spa demons as much as the opposition. He won the British Grand Prix at Aintree and the US Grand Prix at Watkins Glen, all three wins coming with the fastest race lap, and he headed to the final race in East London, South Africa, with a realistic chance of winning the Formula 1 World Championship. Sadly, a bolt came out of the distributor drive housing and the Climax engine jettisoned its oil meaning Clark retired, with the title scooped by Graham Hill.

Few bet against Clark and Lotus for 1963 and with good reason. The Type 25 was the weapon of choice again and the British Racing Green Lotus began the season at Monaco with pole position, although gear selection problems would cause retirement. That was the only retirement, the one time that season that Clark wasn't on the podium as he won at Spa (again) and then Zandvoort. He conquered the daunting French circuit of Reims and delighted home fans at Silverstone. He was second at Nürburgring before winning at Monza and took third at Watkins Glen. Two more wins in Mexico City and East London ended an

Although Clark was a shy man, he couldn't avoid the adulation when he won, such as here at Silverstone in 1963 after a British Grand Prix win.

extraordinary season. To add to the strike rate, Clark mopped up the non-championship Formula 1 races at Silverstone, Oulton Park, Pau, Imola and Karlskoga as well as taking second place in the Indianapolis 500 where the home heroes were baffled and then embarrassed by this strange little rear-engined creation. Clark, in the opinion of many, should have won as he was chasing Parnelli Jones whose Watson-Offenhauser developed an oil leak. Officials had stated that any car dropping oil would be black-flagged, but they prevaricated and Jones took the win,

Chapman unusually not making a fuss as he felt that the car wouldn't make it to the end. Had it been the Lotus leading and dripping oil, some people felt it would have been a different story. However, intent had been served and when Clark won the Milwaukee 200 later in the season, a revolution had begun. He went back in 1964 and led before a rear tyre threw a tread but there was no issue in 1965: he dominated it and took home the $170,000 prize fund. Clark wasn't a fan of Indianapolis as a race but he appreciated the challenge although his 1965 win came at the expense

Colin Chapman, left, and Jim Clark made a formidable combination.

of racing at Monaco which is where he would rather have been. One contemporary report tells of Clark sitting in an airport morose and drinking brandy, dreading the event and the razzamatazz that went with it. For Clark, the appeal was driving cars, not the flummery out of them.

A new car was launched for his 1964 Formula 1 season, the Lotus 33, but it suffered unreliability at many races. Wins still came at Zandvoort and Spa, plus a popular win at Brands Hatch to the delight of the home fans and he took third in the Drivers' Standings. For 1965, in addition to the Indy win, six F1 wins fell to Clark as the 33

won its first six races of the season and put the title, Jimmy's second, out of reach by August. All this came on the back of the popular winter Tasman Series that Jimmy dominated as well and took five wins. He was at the top of his game and with Chapman's engineering ingenuity, the partnership was a special one: Chapman had total faith in Clark's ability behind the wheel and Clark trusted Chapman to give him the tools for the job.

However, in 1966 the Formula 1 regulations had changed by introducing three-litre engines and Chapman was found wanting. A deal had been struck to use BRM H16 engines, but they were late and so Team Lotus began the season with two-litre Climax engines which put Clark in the odd situation of being the underdog as well as reigning world champion. No poles, only one win, moments of frustration. It was the most un-Clark-like of seasons.

For 1967, there was a new car and a new engine. The new chassis was the Type 49 which made its debut at the seaside circuit of Zandvoort where Clark won and notched up a fourth Dutch Grand Prix victory. The new engine was the Cosworth DFV, an engine designed by Keith Duckworth and funded by Ford's Walter Hayes which would go on to dominate the sport for over a decade. The engine wasn't an easy one to master as the power came in with a thump at 6,500 rpm. Progressive power delivery it did not possess.

After Zandvoort, Jimmy won again at Silverstone, Watkins Glen and Mexico and ended the season third but there were standout drives. Take Monza, where he had a puncture and dropped a lap. He fought back, made up the lap and led the race into the last lap when he ran dry of fuel and crossed the line in third. Or Watkins Glen, a race that he won,

but a support broke on the top of his right rear suspension on the last lap, making the wheel fall inwards. He needed to use all of his mechanical sympathy to bring the car to the line with that rear wheel clinging on. He was still six seconds clear at the chequered flag . . .

As Clark's successes had increased, his life had changed too. Expectations that he would marry long-term girlfriend Sally Stokes in 1966 came to nothing as the relationship fizzled out and she married Dutch racing driver Ed Swart. Jimmy threw himself even more into his racing and moved to his new flat in Paris, becoming one of the sport's first tax exiles. That seemed at odds with the quiet, unassuming man from the Scottish hills but the commitment to his motor racing was underlined. Yes, the farm needed to run and would be there when motor racing was finished for him, but now was the time to focus on the sport. To that end, a manager was employed to run the farm.

Clark loved motorsport. In 1964, the year between his Formula 1 titles and one in which he won three grands prix, he won the British Saloon Car Championship driving a Lotus Cortina entered

Clark walks with his Lotus 33-Climax to the grid at Silverstone prior to the 1965 British Grand Prix, which he went on to win.

by Team Lotus, winning outright twice at Oulton Park and Crystal Palace. The title was his with ease. Oulton was also the scene of a remarkable day when he won not only the saloon car race, but a GT race and sports car race as well.

He had a stab at the RAC Rally, Britain's international event. In 1966, at the wheel of a Lotus Cortina (what else?) registered NVW241C, Clark attacked the forests with gusto. With co-driver Brian Melia alongside him, Jim took three special stage wins and was second fastest on a further seven. On stage 40, he went off the road at Loch Achray and damaged the driver's side of the Cortina, but he wasn't set to give up. He rejoined the event but rolled, terminally, on stage 45 at Glengap. He had proved what he was capable of and even after he dropped out, he continued to follow the event by turning up at service halts to offer support to the team.

He raced at Le Mans but didn't enjoy it. He finished third with Roy Salvadori in 1960 in the Border Reivers Aston Martin DBR1/300, then in 1963, he was slated to drive a Lotus 23 but after it failed pre-race scrutineering Clark headed for home. Le Mans as a venue and a race was not for him.

In 1967, Clark made another foray to America to race in NASCAR, a loud, brash and showy form of motor racing that could be no more at odds with Clark's persona. But Jimmy wanted to have a go and struck a deal with the Holman Moody team to drive a Ford Fairlane at Rockingham and as he got himself up to speed, drama struck on the third day of qualifying: he whacked the wall and damaged the car. It was rebuilt and he lined up 25th of the 44 starters and was running 12th before the engine blew. There was no return.

The 1968 season began with the South African Grand Prix at Kyalami where he started from pole in his Lotus 49-Cosworth and he went on to win by 25 seconds. As he pulled into the winner's area post-race, the South African afternoon sunshine picked out the features of a 32-year-old at the height of his powers, but one who looked more relaxed than ever. True, he had a car underneath him capable of winning, but his life in Paris had offered him a taste of the cosmopolitan existence that made it harder to picture him back with his shepherd's crook and wellies. He was popular with the public, that oft-nervous man who chewed his fingernails

and spoke with a soft, Scottish burr. His persona was at odds with his rival of the period, Stirling Moss, who thrived on publicity or fellow Scot Jackie Stewart who was likewise incredibly business-savvy.

And so, with his 25th grand prix win achieved, Jim Clark headed Down Under to tackle the Tasman Series, a winter championship of four races in New Zealand and four in Australia in which he won four races and the title, as he had in 1965 and 1967. He headed next to Barcelona for a Formula 2 race where his newly built Lotus 48 had a monocoque an inch longer than its predecessors. Although he qualified second, Clark retired early having been hit in the rear by Jacky Ickx's Ferrari. Next stop for Clark would be Hockenheim for the *II Deutschland Trophäe* on 7 April, a relatively unimportant race but one that Chapman wanted to win.

Clark hadn't shone in practice and was running eighth in the opening 20-lap heat on a wet day with spray hanging in the air. The Hockenheim circuit, a 4.217-mile circuit not far from Heidelberg, had a twisty stadium section with an almost egg-shaped out-and-back through the forest. It was here, arcing right heading away from the first corner, that Clark's Lotus

Another win, this time the 1967 British Grand Prix as Clark headed for third in the championship.

indestructible. As New Zealander Chris Amon said: 'If it could happen to him, what chance did the rest of us have? It felt as though we had lost our leader.'

Speaking later, Chapman admitted that: 'Jimmy came close to retiring on a couple of occasions and I had mixed feelings about that. The idea of going racing without him was almost unthinkable (but) I loved him as a human being and didn't want him to get hurt. I can't say I've felt the same about (motor racing) since '68.'

In Duns, James Clark Junior's hometown, sits the Jim Clark Room. It sums up the man perfectly: small, almost anonymous, devoid of frills but full of memories and examples of his successes. Almost six decades on, the memory of Clark remains alive, despite the lack of moving footage of the man himself. Rare television interviews give a glimpse of a private man whose career could have achieved so much more but for that wet, miserable day in Germany. He may have railed against the PR and sponsor-driven world, ironically triggered by Lotus and its sponsorship via Gold Leaf that came later in 1968, but he would have

suddenly spun into the trees and he was killed instantly. Drivers that were following him suggested it may have been a mechanical fault, but other suggestions dwelt on a rear tyre failing and spitting Clark off the road. It was a massive blow to Chapman, who hadn't been present, and to the sport as a whole: Clark didn't have a reputation as a crasher, he was safe and gifted and seemed remained a popular man, honest, unassuming and true to his sport.

As later generations ranked Ayrton Senna or Michael Schumacher as the greatest of their era, so Clark's fans rate him as the best, certainly of the 1960s. He became synonymous with Lotus, those beautifully crafted green machines that with their lack of fuss seemed to complement him perfectly and after nine seasons with Colin Chapman's team, 72 F1 races and 25 wins it remains a remarkable strike rate. And that last win came before commercialisation became rampant, making it a fitting end to a quite remarkable era in Formula 1.

Clark, in his Lotus 49-Cosworth won the 1967 British Grand Prix at Silverstone from pole.

Jackie Stewart was Formula 1's first rock star.

5

JACKIE STEWART

Full name	John Young Stewart
Birthdate	11 June 1939
Place of birth	Milton

Jackie Stewart took commercialism to a new level and remained in demand decades after his retirement.

In March 2023, triple world champion Jackie Stewart walked across the podium in Melbourne, trophy in hand. Aged 83, Stewart was there to present the award to the winning team in the Australian Grand Prix, five decades after he retired as a driver. If anyone is immortal in motor racing, it is John Young Stewart.

Ninety-nine grands prix. Three world championships. Wins? 27. Statistics can be made to show anything, but what is astonishing about Sir Jackie Stewart is his longevity. He has been canny in making himself into a brand and was arguably the sport's first true businessman. After his retirement, he picked up a string of broadcasting roles, ambassadorial engagements, ran his own team

in junior single-seater racing, moved it to Formula 1 and then sold it for a song. Stewart has always had an amazing business brain, confounding people who dismissed him at school for his dyslexia. He bounces around a Formula 1 paddock dressed in his trademark Royal Stewart tartan. Yes, a proud Scot but also recognisable, noticeable, memorable. Marketable.

Born in Milton, 15 miles west of Glasgow, motor racing was in the family when Jackie first took an interest, as his brother Jimmy, who was eight years older, raced for the Ecurie Ecosse team. JYS, as his moniker became, was more interested in football and then in clay pigeon shooting at first and won plenty of tournaments and had his eye on a place in the

Stewart's early F1 successes came for BRM until he switched his allegiance to Ken Tyrrell's team.

United Kingdom team in the 1960 Rome Olympics. Sadly, an off day, thanks to admitted complacency, ruined his chances of a place in the team and Stewart consoled himself in a racing car, initially driving an Austin Healey Sprite and then a Marcos in club racing before he followed his older brother and joined Ecurie Ecosse. It was Barry Filer, a customer of the family garage business, who offered Stewart his first drive and watched on as Stewart's natural talent shone, first in the Marcos in which Stewart won four races and then in an Aston Martin DB4GT, before Jackie tested a Jaguar E-type at Oulton Park and matched the lap times of factory driver Roy Salvadori. The floodgates opened: he won races in the E-type and then, for David Murray's Ecurie Ecosse team, there was success aboard a Tojeiro EE Mk2.

In 1964, Stewart was signed for Ecurie Ecosse and tested at Goodwood. Ken Tyrrell, who ran the Cooper Car Company Formula Junior team received a call from the circuit manager waxing lyrical about Stewart. Tyrrell called Jackie's brother, Jimmy, and offered him a test drive. When JYS outpaced incumbent driver Bruce McLaren, Tyrrell offered him a seat on the spot and a remarkable relationship was formed.

Tyrrell moved Stewart straight up to Formula 3 for 1964. The debut was astonishing: at a wet Snetterton, an old airfield circuit in Norfolk, Stewart built a 25-second lead in just two laps before easing home the winner. The winner by 44 seconds, mark you. It was such an impressive drive that Cooper offered Stewart a Formula 1 drive instantly but Jackie refused, opting instead to gain more experience in Formula 3. A win in the Formula 3 race at Monaco added to his reputation and soon Cooper and Tyrrell weren't the only ones watching his progress closely: so too was Lotus boss Colin Chapman who offered Jackie a drive in the non-championship Rand Grand Prix at Kyalami in South Africa. Stewart retired from the first heat when the driveshaft broke on the grid but won the second in style.

Chapman was impressed and offered Stewart a seat in the Lotus Formula 1 team for 1965, but Jackie declined. He would have been paired with Jim Clark and he didn't want to be compared with his fellow Scot and instead signed for BRM to race alongside Graham Hill. In the days of non-championship Formula 1 races, Stewart was runner-up at the Race of Champions held at Brands Hatch and won Silverstone's International Trophy. By the end of the season, he was a grand prix winner as well, Monza being the scene of his maiden triumph. He had battled it out with teammate Hill, Graham running wide late-race and dropping time to Stewart. There was no animosity and Stewart had repaid the faith of imposing team boss Louis Stanley.

The 1966 season was a strange one, beset with lows after early-season highs. He mopped up the Tasman Series held Down Under in the winter months aboard a BRM P261 and won the opening grand prix of the season in Monaco, but then his luck turned: he looked to be a dead cert to win the Indianapolis 500 until his Lola T90's Ford engine failed when he was a lap ahead. On his return to Europe, he had a huge accident at Spa-Francorchamps and his experience of lying in a car soaked in petrol with a broken collarbone and cracked ribs was one that would motivate an unwavering safety campaign. He fully understood how rudimentary the safety and medical provision was: in addition to his injuries was the farce of being taken to a medical tent where little could be done to ease the pain and then a bumpy journey to hospital in a rickety ambulance that got lost en route. Twice . . .

Stewart dedicated himself to improving safety. He would speak, pointedly, of how many funerals he and his wife Helen attended, how many widows they had helped. Some, less focused on safety, rolled their eyes but Stewart was unstoppable in his quest for safety improvements. Just as BRM's Louis Stanley pushed changes and improvements in the medical side, JYS concentrated on the tracks themselves. As Stewart tried to improve circuits for him and his fellow drivers, his credibility was weakened a little by the lack of results as he scored just a fourth and a fifth place after his return to racing. The Spa accident had prompted Stewart to race with a spanner taped inside the cockpit, the easier to release the steering wheel in case of an accident. His detractors pointed

at this and the lack of results and claimed he had lost his bottle.

The 1967 season hardly changed that view, armed, or perhaps saddled, with the BRM chassis using a complex H-16 layout engine. It was ingenious and unreliable in equal measure and results were hard to come by, but Stewart bagged a second place that year. It came at Spa, the scene of his frightening accident the year before and with him needing to hold the car in gear for much of the race. Lost his bottle, you said?

Eventually, Stewart and BRM parted company and his career started to regain momentum. He moved to Ken Tyrrell's team, Uncle Ken now having left Cooper and started on his own. He ran Matra chassis in Formula 2 and was confident that the French firm could make the graduation to Formula 1. Stewart was happy to go with Tyrrell's decision: after all, he knew the team and knew what Matra could do. It turned out to be a good decision as Jackie won the third race of the season in Holland armed not only with an effective chassis but Dunlop tyres and the Ford-Cosworth DFV engine that was at the top of its game. Two more race wins came, one at the Nürburgring which was

Jackie Stewart's win in a wet 1968 German Grand Prix was one of his finest. His Matra MS10-Cosworth won by over four minutes.

perhaps his finest drive. It was wet and misty, awful conditions for racing especially on the 14-mile, tree-lined circuit. Stewart hit the front and drove away from the opposition. He finished the race four minutes ahead of anyone else. He was at the podium before runner-up Hill had pierced the gloom and taken the chequered flag. That year Stewart finished as runner-up in the title race, and a year later he went one better to take his first world championship. Armed with the beautiful Matra MS80, Stewart was the benchmark driver with wins in South Africa, Spain, Holland, France, Great

Britain and Italy. It was a car that JYS loved driving and it suited his style perfectly but no sooner had his title success been achieved than a problem loomed: the Cosworth DFV engine was the powerplant to have but politics meant that Matra could no longer use an engine funded by a rival motor manufacturer, namely Ford. That meant that Ken Tyrrell's team had a choice of what to keep, engines or chassis. Ken opted for the engine and therefore had to buy a chassis from elsewhere. He opted for a March 701 and Stewart did his best but it was a dreadful car and although Jackie took a win in Spain, it was a false dawn as there

He was at the top of his game, and the Tyrrell/ Stewart axis was a strong one, Ken providing Jackie with everything he needed.

was no development over the season and one owner, Andy Granatelli, converted the tub of his car into a flowerbox. Ken Tyrrell went one better and built his own car that was debuted at the non-championship Oulton Park Gold Cup before being taken to world championship races.

For 1971, Stewart and Tyrrell came out fighting starting with second in South Africa and wins started to fall like skittles: Spain, Monaco, France, Britain, Germany and Canada all had Stewart atop the podium as Jackie took a second world championship. He was at the top of his game, and the Tyrrell/ Stewart axis was a strong one, Ken providing Jackie with everything he needed. The 001, 002 and 003 models were used during the season and Jackie went into 1972 in a confident mood. When he won the opening race in Argentina, it looked like business as usual but a spin in Spain and another in Monaco suggested that something was amiss.

An ulcer was diagnosed and he was forced to sit out the Belgian Grand Prix while it was removed, but he was back at his best on his return taking three more wins before the end of the season. Even with four retirements and skipping the Belgian race, he was still placed second in the championship and raring to go for 1973.

Stewart entered the season in a confident mood and, with the Tyrrell 005 and a Cosworth DFV engine, there were five more wins as he went up against Lotus with the Type 72 chassis for young Brazilian talent Emerson Fittipaldi and teammate Ronnie Peterson. They did their best but Stewart, even aboard a nervous car like the Tyrrell, had their measure.

Early in 1973, Jackie Stewart the racing driver, the then double world champion, started to think about life after motor racing. He had been a regular on television thanks to his successes and was in demand as an ambassador for large corporations. He had been the subject of a documentary by film-maker Roman Polanski and with the long hair and sunglasses the Scotsman looked as much a cool rock star as a racing driver. He wanted a third title but he also wanted out when the time was right and early in '73 he announced his decision to Tyrrell and Ford's motorsport supremo Walter Hayes: this would be his last season. With his teammate Francois Cevert, life at Tyrrell was good that year. They got on well, Cevert happy to learn from the master and play the team game at the same time, such as in Germany that year when he sacrificed his own speed to follow home Stewart and help his world championship aspirations. Stewart was content to hand over the baton at Tyrrell to Cevert for 1974.

Stewart won the 1971 British Grand Prix at Silverstone, his Tyrrell 003-Cosworth heading for the title.

Stewart at speed at Monaco where he took three wins.

The final race of 1973 was to be Stewart's 100th grand prix and was held at Watkins Glen outside New York. He qualified sixth before silence fell over the circuit: Cevert had crashed heavily having lost control on a bumpy part of the circuit and hurtled through the barriers with such force that he stood no chance of survival. Stewart withdrew from the race and hence his career stood at 99 races, although he didn't announce his retirement until three days after attending Cevert's funeral. It was an irony that the sport's great safety crusader should have his career cut short, albeit by just one race, by a tragedy that took his own teammate and made his quest to make the sport safer look unsuccessful. In truth, Cevert's death illustrated just how important his task was and how the sport has never stood still in its bid to make it safer.

There was more to Stewart than just single-seaters as during his time in F1 he found weekends to race, for example, Ford Capris in the European Touring Car Championship, Can-Am sports cars in the United States, had occasional outings in the British Saloon Car Championship and raced at Le Mans sharing the Rover-BRM gas turbine entry with Graham Hill.

He retired aged 34 and channelled his energies into other areas. He was never tempted by a comeback, nor the money that went with it, and instead racked up endless commercial associations. Always fit, Stewart was never a smoker, only an occasional drinker and the fitness behind the wheel was replaced by a boundless energy for organisations. There was television commentary work, not just on motor racing but on the luge at the 1976 Winter Olympics and equestrian at the Summer Olympics for ABC in America. There were books, public speaking engagements and a promotional role for Ford that lasted for decades, adding among others Heineken, RBS and Rolex.

In the late 1980s, Stewart's elder son Paul decided to follow in his father's footsteps and start racing. The pair formed Paul

He was never tempted by a comeback, nor the money that went with it, and instead racked up endless commercial associations.

Stewart Racing, initially to run Paul in Formula Vauxhall Lotus and then Formula 3 before he moved into Formula 3000, eventually retiring as a driver at the end of 1993. The team, PSR, had become a powerhouse in junior single-seater racing especially in Formula Vauxhall and Formula 3, with an impressive list of drivers and successes. Eventually, Paul and Jackie decided that they only had one more category to aim for, Formula 1. For 1997, Stewart Grand Prix was in the F1 paddock but the car was uncompetitive and, despite a healthy budget from Ford, limited progress was made a year later. In 1999, though, the toil became worthwhile when Johnny Herbert splashed through the Nürburgring rain to claim Stewart Grand Prix's only win, but the struggles to be competitive had impacted on Stewart and the team was sold to Ford for 2000 and rebranded as Jaguar Racing before Ford sold it and it became Red Bull Racing.

Stewart knew the risks, wasn't afraid of taking them but knew how to manage them and . . . the sport owes him a huge debt for making circuits safer.

Stewart was president of the British Racing Drivers' Club and never missed a chance to bang the drum about the importance of motorsport to the UK economy nor the huge role a British Grand Prix played, especially at a time when contract negotiations between Silverstone and Bernie Ecclestone were difficult. Stewart was chairman of the Grand Prix Mechanics Trust for 30 years, the aim to provide for the unsung heroes of the pit lane and in 2018, after his wife since 1962, Helen, was diagnosed with dementia, he established the Race Against Dementia charity hoping to use Formula 1 technology and radical thinking to bring earlier solutions to people struggling with the condition.

To say that Jackie Stewart retired at the end of 1973 is almost a fib. Sure, he never raced again but he is as busy as ever, in demand for an autograph, an opinion or a memory wherever he goes at a race. Not

everyone appreciated his opinions, though, such as FIA president Max Mosley who, in 2007, described him as a 'certified halfwit' and 'a figure of fun'. 'Some members of the British motorsport establishment consider Jackie Stewart to be a national treasure,' said Mosley. 'I have known Jackie for almost 40 years, and understand their view, but they must forgive me if I do not share it.' Seemingly, most people disagree with Mosley as, in 2023, Stewart strides the paddock still, punctual, professional, respected.

Never in his career did he spill blood. Broken bones, yes, but never blood and that was at a time when the sport was at its most dangerous. Stewart knew the risks, wasn't afraid of taking them but knew how to manage them and despite the criticism received at the time, the sport owes him a huge debt for making circuits safer. Now there are run-off areas not walls, gravel traps not trees and fatalities are thankfully rare.

As a person, Stewart worked hard on his image when driving and looked at opportunities for the future. Louis Stanley wrote in his book *Behind the Scenes* of Stewart, that: 'Jackie has always been over-talkative. He can't help it. Words just

Jackie Stewart's victory in the 1972 Canadian Grand Prix at Mosport Park was the 50th win for the Cosworth DFV engine.

gush out.' It was that ability to talk to anyone, royalty included, that made his contact book the envy of the paddock. He had no trouble attracting backers for his teams and today with emails and mobile phones controlling his schedule, he remains as passionate as ever for the sport that has given him so much.

Awarded an Order of the British Empire in 1972, he was knighted in 2001 and shows no signs of

Jackie Stewart ran junior single-seater teams before graduating to Formula 1. Stewart Grand Prix lasted just three seasons but achieved a race win. Rubens Barrichello, seen here at Monaco, drove for the team every year.

slowing down. The tartan cap and trousers remain an integral part of the paddock and of his brand, making sure that a new generation of fans know who he is and what his legacy in the sport involves.

Think about this: not one driver in the current F1 entry was born during Jackie Stewart's career as a driver, but they all know him, they all respect him and they all know what he has done in the sport. That is an amazing accolade. Five decades on from his last grand

prix, Jackie Stewart remains in the Formula 1 paddock, the elder statesman and yet the enthusiast, the ambassador, the triple world champion. Few have had such an association with the sport, few have achieved as much as him and few have thrown themselves into as many roles as Stewart has.

With what Sir Jackie Stewart OBE has achieved on and off the track, describing him in a soundbite is almost impossible. Let's agree on one thing: he's truly unforgettable.

Sir Jackie Stewart retired from driving at the end of 1973 as the world champion, but never left the sport.

Derek Bell made a name for himself in the 1970s as he rose to the ranks of Ferrari drivers but his career seemed to stall before sports car racing came knocking.

6

DEREK BELL

Full name	Derek Reginald Bell
Birthdate	31 October 1941
Place of birth	Pinner

A successful sports car career made Derek Bell
revered, especially in Porsches with which he
enjoyed five Le Mans 24 Hour victories.

For the 2023 Le Mans 24 Hours, the centenary race, British driver Alex Lynn painted his crash helmet in Derek Bell's colours. 'The thing about Derek is he's achieved so much, hehas legendary status, but he is such a cool guy too. He's the UK's most successful Le Mans racer and drove so many iconic cars with so many iconic drivers. He is everything we all dream of, he is why we want to compete in this race in the first place.' That sums up Derek Bell in a nutshell.

Think Derek Bell and you think sports car racing, most likely Le Mans and Porsche. And yet, despite five wins in the French 24-hour classic, three in the Daytona 24 Hours and two World Sportscar Championship title wins, there is far more to Bell than just that impression. To pigeonhole him as a sports car racer fails to give credit to his versatility, having raced in everything from Formula 1 to one-make saloons, and his irrepressible enthusiasm as Bell remains as keen as ever on the sport he loves, performing the role of Grand Marshal at the 2021 Le Mans 24 Hours, for example, at the age of 79. He has raced and rallied in a hugely varied career.

Derek Reginald Bell wasn't born into a motor racing family. His parents divorced when he was nine and his mother remarried. His stepfather, Bernard Hinder, was known to everyone as 'The Colonel' and allowed young Derek

Derek Bell (March 712M) heads Peter Westbury in Mallory Park's non-championship Formula 2 race in 1971. He would be classified 12th.

to drive tractors on the family farm before allowing him to get behind the wheel of his high-performance road cars. Bell recalls driving The Colonel's Jaguar XK150 to the 1957 Italian Grand Prix and nudging 115 mph before the dozing Hinder awoke to tell him to slow down. He was a huge supporter of Derek's racing, financing much of his early career and suggesting that he give up farming to concentrate on his racing.

Bell's motor racing story began in 1964 when he drove a Lotus Seven in club racing events and then moved up to Formula 3 in an elderly Lotus 31 run by Church Farm Racing which was effectively the family team. By Derek's admission,

it sounded grander than it was. Derek accumulated spare parts if not results: he suffered a sizeable accident at Enna in Sicily when he finished upside down and at the French street circuit of Pau he careered off the road between the trees and emerged sitting in a wheel-free tube. In 1967, though, Derek's fortunes changed as he became part of a three-car team of Brabham BT21s in Formula 3 and the results soon came with third in the coveted Monaco Grand Prix support race and then a win at Zolder. To add to his CV and start the versatility that would be a subplot to his career, Derek also tackled the Ollon-Villars hillclimb in France in which he took a class win. Now the British motorsport press was taking note of the young Englishman.

Derek knew that he had to move up to Formula 2 for 1968 but money was an issue. The Colonel had funded the first three seasons of his career but had to draw a line somewhere and it meant that Bell had to raise the funding himself for his F2 bow. By selling his F3 Brabham, he raised £3000 but against £2500 for a new Brabham BT23C for F2, that wasn't going to stretch far. However, Derek's determination impressed The Colonel once more and he stepped in to help with funding for one more season. His second F2 race was at Hockenheim and one that affected him and everyone else who was there: Jim Clark was killed. Derek's idol was gone and although he had known tragedy in F3, this was the one accident that made Derek, and others, ask if they wanted to be a racing driver.

He did. His season continued apace with more F2 races as the travelling band criss-crossed Europe. As the results started to come in F2, Derek's career had a boost as Ferrari asked him to race its F2 Dino 166S, and against a paltry offer from Cooper to drive its cars, Derek accepted the *lire*. His first race as a Ferrari driver was the prestigious Monza Lottery F2 Grand Prix and Derek impressed by qualifying on pole position. Come the race, he was in the leading bunch but had a big spin exiting the Parabolica corner that wiped out a pack of cars including the rest of the Ferrari team. In spite of this, Enzo Ferrari was impressed enough to sign Derek to race in the F2 Dino at Tulln-Langenlebarn and then came the offer to race a Formula 1 Ferrari in the non-championship Gold Cup race at Oulton Park in which he retired with gearbox problems. But in just four seasons, he had gone from racing rookie to Ferrari factory driver. Impressive indeed.

Next came his grand prix debut as Derek was back on the Monza grid for the Italian race, an excellent qualifying effort putting him eighth on the grid although his race ended after four laps when a piston blew when he was running seventh.

The momentum slowed the following season. Although Derek raced for Ferrari in the Tasman Series in Australia and New Zealand at the start of the year, his programme for the season was just to drive for Ferrari in Formula 2 again but as the company was in financial straits and set to be taken over by Fiat, long-term planning wasn't an option. Instead, Derek moved to race a McLaren M9A in the British Grand Prix at Silverstone, his first appearance in his home race. Suspension problems put him out and it would be his sole grand prix for Bruce McLaren's eponymous team. As his Ferrari deal had come to an end as well, Derek's career had seemingly hit the blocks, a far cry from the previous season when Ferrari was on the phone. Instead, he turned to Leicestershire builder and arch-enthusiast Tom Wheatcroft who was happy to help and assisted Derek in buying an ex-works Brabham BT26A for the 1970 Tasman Series but Wheatcroft had a close relationship with Dunlop and hence ran the car on its tyres, whereas the chassis had been designed to run on Goodyears. It meant Derek struggled and two engine failures also blighted his Tasman attack. Back in Europe, F2 beckoned once more with Wheatcroft and it was a year that re-ignited Derek's career as he finished second in the European F2 title race. He stayed with Wheatcroft for 1971 in which Tom ran him in non-championship races at the start of the season and further F1 outings followed for Wheatcroft and John

When Derek and Jo won the 1971 World Sports Car Championship opening race in Buenos Aires, it looked as though a good season was on the cards.

Surtees up to 1974. The trouble was that after racing for Ferrari, Derek was no longer seen as up-and-coming and hence soon dropped off teams' shopping lists. Indeed, when Enzo Ferrari was asked why he didn't use Bell again for single-seater races, his answer was: 'I never re-heat cold soup.' Derek admitted it was a crushing remark and left him at a crossroads in his career.

In 1971, Derek Bell sports car racer was born and a whole new, successful chapter would be written. Derek joined John Wyer's Gulf-sponsored team to drive a Porsche 917 with Jo Siffert, Derek having come to Wyer's notice after two outings in Ferraris in 1969, at Spa in a private entry and Le Mans in a factory car. When Derek and Jo won the 1971 World Sports Car Championship opening race in Buenos Aires, it looked as though a good season was on the cards, although it turned out to be their only win and teammates Jackie

Derek's time with the Broadspeed-run Jaguars was frustrating. Here at Monza in 1977, oil pressure dramas would force retirement.

Oliver and Pedro Rodriguez headed for title glory. Once again, Derek was in demand and was busy in 1972. There was a season driving Wyer's Gulf-liveried Mirage in World Sports Car Championship races, an Osella in the 2-litre sports car scene and a return to Formula 1. After David Yorke had left Wyer's sports car team, he was employed by Martini and Rossi as a consultant to its F1 ambitions and he advised them to join Bernie Ecclestone's Brabham team and take Derek

with them. Instead, the Italian drink maker was wowed by Luciano Perdazini, the Tecno constructor. He sold an idea of an Italian car with an Italian sponsor taking on and beating Ferrari. Martini and Rossi were hooked and Derek returned to the F1 grid. Well, occasionally: twice he didn't qualify the recalcitrant car, once it didn't start after a crash in the morning warm up and he retired from the two races he started. In his book *My Racing Life* Derek described the experience as 'gruesome'. A few outings for Surtees came in 1974 but they were doomed as well as the car was off the pace.

In 1975, Derek Bell became a rather peripatetic driver, grabbing a seat where and when he could. It enhanced his reputation as a sports car racer but thanks to his error-free style and mechanical sympathy he became a go-to driver for a variety of teams. A Campari-liveried Alfa Romeo T33 took Derek to honours in the Spa 1000 kilometres but he had also signed a deal to drive for Gulf in a Mirage M8 at Le Mans sharing with Jacky Ickx who had asked team owner John Wyer if he could share with Derek and it was the start of a successful relationship with the generous Belgian. He insisted that Bell start and finish the race as he was the one who had done the development work on the car. Such teammates are hard to find . . .

Success at Le Mans came in 1981 when Derek shared the Porsche 936/81 with Jacky Ickx. The car took the lead before nightfall and won easily.

Running a detuned engine to save fuel and help reliability, Derek and Jacky led despite an awful noise afflicting their car. After a long stop to replace a cracked exhaust manifold, they held on to win by a lap and post-race the car was stripped to reveal the graunching noise: one of the rear suspension pick-up points on the gearbox casing had fractured but when the car was at rest and the team was able to check it, the offending part dropped back into place and the damage remained undetected. Mechanical sympathy prevailed and Derek's first Le Mans win came. In 1981, the Bell/Ickx partnership won again as their Porsche 936 breezed through the race trouble-free. Derek's relationship with Porsche was already strong, having raced a 924 Turbo as well as the 917, and for 1982 he was asked by the factory to become part of its new sports car programme. The FIA, the sport's governing body, launched new regulations called Group C and Porsche launched a landmark car, the 956. In its Rothmans colours, the car soon hit its stride in Group C races and headed to Le Mans looking for a win. Derek shared with Ickx again but they were delayed by a fuel mixture problem early on and

lost time. They eventually battled their way back into contention. By x1 am on Sunday they were back in the lead and headed to victory. The following year, Derek was hit by the lows of Le Mans as he and Ickx were delayed on lap two after Jacky tangled with Jan Lammers' Porsche. It took 14 hours to get into the lead and as soon as he had done so, Derek's engine cut out. He effected repairs and they finished second.

More Le Mans successes came in 1986 and 1987, against increasingly significant Jaguar opposition, his latter two wins coming with Al Holbert and Hans-Joachim Stuck after Ickx hung up his helmet. In '85, Bell and Stuck (or BEST as the pit board abbreviated their partnership) won the World Endurance Championship and in 1986 they won the newly-titled World Sports-Prototype Championship, although this came about thanks to a lot of determination on Derek's part as Porsche didn't want to do the Brands Hatch round and so a Joest team car had to be hired at a cost of £35,000 to put Bell and Stuck on the grid. It seemed a poor way to treat the reigning world champions . . .

While Derek was busy racing and winning for Porsche in Europe, a parallel career was being forged in America. He had raced Bob Akin's Red Lobster Racing BMW M1 in 1980 and he joined Akin in his Coca-Cola Porsche 935 for the '81 Daytona 24 Hours in which they finished second and more American outings soon followed for a variety of Porsche owners, some cars more competitive than others. Derek, though, was pragmatic: bills needed paying back home. In 1984, Derek received a phone call from a PR contact who was handling the Löwenbräu brand, owned in the USA by Marlboro. A deal was struck to put Derek and Al Holbert on the IMSA Sports Car grid in a Löwenbräu-sponsored Porsche 962 with which they took third in the championship and then won it outright a year later with six wins. Between them, Bell and Holbert made a fine duo, both fast, error-free and without egos needing to be boosted. In addition, Derek took wins in the Daytona 24 Hours in 1986, 1987 and 1989 as his reputation Stateside increased and he spent more time racing across the pond than in Europe.

By 1988, Porsche's spell in Group C racing was at an end, as a factory at least. They fielded a Le Mans programme which went badly for Derek as co-driver Klaus Ludwig tried to go one extra lap on a tank

of fuel and ran dry, costing their car two laps. They finished second, but long after Derek regarded it as the one that got away. After that, more Le Mans drives came but never at quite the same level. There were outings in privateer Porsche 962s, one of note being the 1992 race when Derek shared his ADA Engineering car with his son Justin, along with Tiff Needell. In the wet, and in a car set up for the dry, they battled to 12th but it gave dad great pleasure to share a car with his lad. They would do so again in 1995 in the new era of GT cars at Le Mans when they joined 1988 winner Andy Wallace in a Harrods-sponsored McLaren F1-GTR. They led for 16 hours, Derek outpacing the chasing JJ Lehto in one stint even though he was now in his fifties but transmission dramas delayed them late in the race and they finished third. It was Derek's final Le Mans 24 Hours and fittingly it resulted in a podium.

So, Bell was handy in a single-seater and a star in a sports car. End of story? No. There was success, too, in touring car racing, with a win in a BMW CSL in the 1973 Tourist Trophy, Silverstone's event run over two heats with Derek and co-driver Harald Ertl each winning their two-

A lap two crash and stopping trackside to reattach a wire in the electrical circuit hurt Derek's chances of a 1983 Le Mans win. Two laps behind with 40 minutes to go, he was 64 seconds off the lead at the end of 24 hours of racing.

hour race. That led to Derek being approached by Jaguar to race its XJ Coupe in the 1976 European Touring Car Championship. The red, white and blue Big Cat was prepared by Ralph Broad whose Broadspeed concern had a good reputation for preparing saloon cars, but the project, in Derek's words: 'Was a fiasco from start to finish.' British Leyland had high hopes and unveiled the XJ as: 'The car with which we are going to win the European Touring Car Championship round at Salzburgring in three weeks.' Bell was alarmed and when he drove the car the concerns mounted. The rear

axle regularly overheated, the brakes were poor and the engine had dramatic oil surge dramas. Wheels fell off, both in testing and racing such as the Tourist Trophy for which Derek had qualified on pole. Things were no better for 1977, partly because Jaguar wouldn't decide if it were carrying on or not and hence Broadspeed didn't know whether to spend money and time developing the car. A second at Nürburgring should have been mirrored by second at Silverstone until Derek's co-driver Andy Rouse lobbed the car off the road nine laps from home.

Derek wasn't one to turn down a drive, partly for financial

reasons with a family to support, but also thanks to his passion for driving. Take 1979 when in addition to his IMSA races in America he drove in the UK's BMW County Championship, a one-make series in BMW 323is representing different dealers from the regions. There was also an outing at the fabled Australian circuit of Bathurst where he shared Phil McDonnell's Alfa Romeo GTV to 10th place and second in class. He was back two years later and was third with Allan Moffat in a Mazda RX-7. That same year, 1981, in which, remember, he had won Le Mans, he won the historic sports car race at the British Grand Prix aboard a Porsche 917. Oh, and there was a crack at rallying as well, when Derek tackled the 1987 Lombard RAC Rally in a Vauxhall Astra and on the live

The 1988 Le Mans 24 Hours was a race that Derek Bell felt he could have won, but for co-driver Klaus Ludwig running dry of fuel early in the race.

television stage had the engine drown as he went into a water splash. The car rejoined, only for a bent con rod to blow the engine. A year later he came back for another crack in snowy conditions and battled to 27th place.

Derek was also involved in the making of Steve McQueen's Le Mans movie driving a Ferrari but he suffered the worst injury of his career when the car erupted into flames during a filming sequence, leaving Derek with minor facial burns.

Part of his longevity is his personality. Loquacious, patient, pleasant, professional. It is small wonder that Bentley recruited him as an ambassador when it announced a return to international motor racing in 2001 and why broadcasters and corporations have called upon his services. He has been a popular after-dinner speaker and an incisive commentator after decades of observing the sport.

Twice married, Derek is an American green card carrier and married Misti in 1998. His first marriage to Pam fizzled out in the late 1980s when Derek admits to being so focused on his racing that he neglected family life. His son, Justin, through his first marriage, called

Porsche gave Derek Bell huge success. In 2017 he was commemorated with a British Legends model of the 911 Carrera 4 GTS.

time on his racing career before becoming another proficient analyst of the sport for television. A second son, Sebastian, was born in 1999.

Five times a Le Mans 24 Hour winner, three times a Daytona 24 winner, twice a World Sports Car Champion and four times a winner of the British Racing Drivers' Club's Gold Star, Derek Bell was awarded an MBE in 1986 for services to motor racing. But more than that he has proven that there is life outside Formula 1 and a good life too.

When Porsche launched a range of special edition 911 Carrera 4 GTS models in 2017, they were named after British winners in a Porsche at Le Mans. There were just three names. One, of course, was Derek Bell's. To be immortalised on a Porsche . . . now, there is an accolade.

Gerry Marshall and Baby Bertha, one of the most successful double acts of the 1970s.

Full name	Gerald Dallas (Royston) Marshall
Birthdate	16 November 1941 (died 21 April 2005)
Place of birth	St Neots

A hard-charging Gerry Marshall was a sight to behold
as he dominated British national events in his pomp.
Racer, rival and friend, he helped many along the way.

In the 1970s, it was impossible to miss Gerry Marshall. It wasn't just his skill behind the wheel or his sideways approach to a racetrack, but his larger-than-life personality and penchant for a pint that made him a fan favourite. When he died behind the wheel of a Chevrolet Camaro on a track day in 2005, he had racked up 625 wins from a career that spanned over 1400 races, rallies or sprints.

Gerald Dallas Royston Marshall, the 'Royston' being added by Gerry many years after his birth, was a truly remarkable man. Not for nothing was he known as Big Gerry, but woe betide anyone who fell for thinking he was big and slow: a favourite trick was to put money on the bar and challenge someone to a running sprint. He would always win and that was largely down to quick reactions when someone yelled 'Go!' which he reckoned was why he always made amazing starts behind the wheel of a racing car.

His career really began in Minis, like so many in the 1960s, but by the 1970s he had achieved celebrity status with a string of successful Vauxhalls in national racing, before racing Triumphs, Fords, Opels . . . we could be here all day.

The Marshall story began in 1961 when he entered a sprint, but the entry was over-subscribed and he didn't get to compete until October that year. It was 1964 when he first went circuit racing with an Austin A35 and then his first Mini. During the 1963 to

Marshall's Jaguar Mk2 2.4 heads the similar car of Bob Meacham at Silverstone where Gerry triumphed in a Classic Saloon Car Championship thrash.

1965 seasons, Gerry tackled 40 events aboard Minis and took 16 class wins, no mean achievement for a big man in a little car with a significant weight disadvantage but having proved himself to be a force to be reckoned with, he took the step up to more powerful machinery, which started to make the Marshall story. Gerry in a rear-wheel drive car, sideways, would become the stuff of legend.

He went to work, briefly, for the Barnet Motor Company owned by Martin Lilley who would also own TVR. He put Marshall in TVR models for autocross, sprinting and racing and wins came in all. He worked as sales manager for Barnet and that led him to drive the firm's Lotus Elans as well, his first outing being in a sprint with the 1650cc car carrying the registration number BAR 1. What else? After leaving BarMoCo and starting his own company manufacturing glass fibre parts for MGB owners, Marshall rekindled a relationship with a man for whom he had tested a Mini back in 1966, Dutch-Norwegian Anglophile Bill Blydenstein. Engineer Bill had become the leader of Dealer Team Vauxhall (DTV) and was charged with turning Vauxhall's products into competition winners. Marshall was the ideal man to help achieve the aims, not just on-track but also maximising the firm's PR potential.

Blydenstein started the Vauxhall-Marshall era with the Viva, a dull, small, booted family saloon that generated a far from exciting 80 bhp from its 1159cc engine. Blydenstein soon had it kicking out 95 bhp from a bored-and-stroked 1265cc engine and the car hit the track in 1967 although results didn't really come until 1968 when Vauxhall was able to use a 2-litre slant four-cylinder engine from parent company General Motors and that, plus fuel injection, transformed the Viva GT. Initially, it was a martyr to understeer, but

Blydenstein and Gerry gradually sorted the car and it was a winner by the summer. Marshall and the Viva kept on racking up class wins, but for 1971 there was a new model that Vauxhall wanted to promote and it was the Firenza, a car that would be dubbed 'Old Nail', but it was a while before Marshall had that car to his liking. In the meantime, Gerry had made BBC television viewers sit up and take notice during a televised race at Crystal Palace in 1971, an event initially led by Martin Thomas (Chevrolet Camaro) which slithered off the road allowing Mike Crabtree's Ford Escort to lead from Gerry's Viva, but Crabtree had jumped the start and so Marshall cannily sat close enough behind to benefit from the inevitable penalty. In November, the Firenza made its debut at Lydden Hill in front of the BBC cameras once more and Marshall won the race which made up for DTV teammates Roger

Initially, it was a martyr to understeer, but Blydenstein and Gerry gradually sorted the car and it was a winner by the summer.

Bell and Mike Crabtree crashing their Vivas into each other!

The Firenza really made its name by gaining backing from Thames Television, then the London-based regional ITV service. With a 2-litre engine and 127 bhp on tap, it was a quick car made quicker for competition use and the Special Saloon category was chosen to showcase the car as levels of modification were greater and thus it could be made to go faster which explains why a 2.5-litre engine was squeezed under the bonnet and 214 bhp came out of it! Marshall was a force to be reckoned with as win after win came, Vauxhall's active PR machine backing up the on-track successes, and the win rate continued through 1972 and 1973, a year in which Gerry pleased the sponsors by taking the Thames Television-backed car to a win in the *TV Times*-sponsored Race of the Stars meeting at Brands Hatch.

By 1974, Vauxhall was looking to promote other models, the big four-door Ventora being on the list, and so 'Old Nail' was parked after 47 outright and 63 class wins. The Ventora, debuted in 1974, was given the moniker 'Big Bertha' and it was a whale of a car built by Blydenstein for the Super Saloon series for even more modified saloon cars where horsepower and engine size grew and the cars sprouted more aerodynamic aids. The racing version was launched with Marshall and topless models posed by the silver car and its first race was at Silverstone in March where Marshall took it to a win. Two more followed but its sixth race was its last as the mighty V8 Repco Holden-engined car suffered a massive accident at Silverstone when Gerry tried to beat Australian Frank Gardner. The car's brake pads had not been wire-locked in place and fell out under heavy braking. The car was a sorry sight and the decision was made to build the internals into a new car, this time something more manageable than the huge saloon. Enter 'Baby Bertha', a much-modified Firenza with a Chevrolet-Holden engine capable of 0-60 mph in 4.2 seconds and wins fell like skittles to the car-engineer-driver combination. Fans loved the car and its spectacular look, allied to the charismatic man behind the wheel whose flamboyant driving style made dull races exciting. And there were dull ones, Marshall and Baby Bertha being too good for the opposition, and ultimately their dominance sounded the death knell for the Super Saloon

Fans loved the car and its spectacular look, allied to the charismatic man behind the wheel whose flamboyant driving style made dull races exciting.

category as defeated rivals went elsewhere. Over 30 race wins went to Gerry and Baby Bertha, but by 1977 things were changing . . .

Motor dealers Tricentrol had moved its sponsorship from Super Saloons to the British Saloon Car

A kerb-hopping Marshall bounces his Vauxhall Magnum through Silverstone's Woodcote chicane in 1976.

'Old Nail' was Gerry's hugely successful Special Saloon Vauxhall Firenza. Here, he heads for glory at Oulton Park.

Championship and this is where Vauxhall wanted to be with the Magnum coupe model. Marshall raced Baby Bertha just five times in 1977 and the relationship signed off with a win at Thruxton, but Marshall needed to think of the future and it would be without Vauxhall. That '77 season, though, had generated a tremendous result for Gerry in the touring car Spa 24 Hours in which he shared a Magnum with Australian hero Peter Brock. They had teamed up the year before at Silverstone, although the car suffered brake dramas, but at Spa they shone. Second place was the result but when Gerry went to Bathurst that October for the return leg, he was very disappointed to find that he wouldn't share with Brock but with Basil van Rooyen and he would suffer assorted dramas including seat mounting failures and even an electrical drama triggered by short-circuiting everything on the grid when he tested the radio. 'I gave Brock the best everything,' he told me. 'The best car, the best women . . .' Gerry's son Gregor confirmed to Jeremy Walton

He suffered facial and head cuts, three skull fractures, cracked ribs and what he described as 'Assaults on my jaw, teeth and kidney'.

in his authorised biography of Marshall that: 'Even in the week he died [he] commented on his dislike of Peter Brock.' Whoever at Goodwood thought it was appropriate, therefore, to let Brock drive Baby Bertha at the Festival of Speed was ignorant to say the least.

Marshall moved into the British Saloon Car Championship's main class for 1978 when the series was split into four classes based on engine size. In a three-litre Ford Capri in Triplex colours, he had a tough season with a number of retirements, but there was a secondary programme with Triumph Dolomite Sprints that offered better fortunes. The angular-looking, four-door cars achieved decent results in 1978 in Production Saloons but hopes of a successful 1979 in the BSCC were met with an opponent that Marshall resented: Tom Walkinshaw and the Mazda RX-7. It wasn't Walkinshaw *per se* that

annoyed Gerry, but his success in convincing rule-makers that the two-door coupe with its rotary engine was actually a touring car. It meant that Gerry had to drive the wheels off his Dolly, often needing a pit stop as he had worked the tyres so hard and it all came to a head at Silverstone in July 1979 when Marshall was ahead of Walkinshaw approaching the fast right hander of Club Corner in the British Grand Prix support race. Contact was made, accidentally or otherwise, and Marshall's car cartwheeled off the road. He suffered facial and head cuts, three skull fractures, cracked ribs and what he described as 'Assaults on my jaw, teeth and kidney'. He needed stitches in his face and spent a couple of months out of the cockpit as he recovered. Marshall would suffer decades later from back injuries sustained in the frightening crash and worse was that not only was he not winning, but on the horizon was a contract from British Leyland to run the Rover SD1 programme in the BSCC for 1980 and Gerry wanted that, *needed* that. That it would ultimately go to Walkinshaw rubbed salt into the wounds. The 1979 season

'Baby Bertha' guided Gerry to 20 wins in the 24 races in which he drove it and cemented his reputation.

that began with such optimism and hope, turned out to be one of the worst of Gerry's career.

Marshall, though, loved racing. And he loved racing anything. Thus, he started to drive in historic events in 1980, first in a Lister Jaguar, then a Lola T70, then an Aston Martin DBR4, the company's Formula 1 effort from 1959. With the Lola, he won the Marlboro Cup Super Sports race at the 1981 Dubai Grand Prix, the first motor racing event in the Emirate state and it began a parallel career as he continued to race for the next two decades. Gone, though, was his time in the top level of saloon car racing, the

BSCC. Instead, he became one of the leading lights in the second-tier Production Saloon category, and with Autoplan's support, mopped up the 1981 season in the new Ford Capri 2.8i. He continued to race Capris in 1982 as well as adding to his historic racing successes and returned to Lotus in 1983 by racing an Esprit Turbo in Production Sports Car events.

Stories of Marshall and pubs are numerous, such as qualifying in the morning and going to the pub at lunchtime before returning to race and win in the afternoon, but his hard-drinking persona reared its head in November 1983 when he

Gerry Marshall and his beloved 'Baby Bertha', sideways. All three elements added up to successes aplenty in the 1970s.

More success came aboard a Ford Capri 2.8i. Here, at Silverstone in 1982, Gerry heads his good mate Graham Scarborough on his way to another win.

lost his road licence after hitting another car after a rather long night with Beaujolais Nouveau. It meant that he did just a part season in '84 and had to sit out '85 altogether, in which time he concentrated on team ownership and business deals.

Always a man with an eye for a deal, Marshall achieved varying levels of success with his car dealing ventures. Some had succeeded, others folded quickly and he had formed a new team for 1986 to run cars in ProdSaloons. Marshall started the season in an Opel Monza, but

he soon discovered it was breathless against the Mitsubishi Starion Turbos that were the cars to have and hence switched to a Ford Escort RS Turbo mid-season. That year, he carried an on-board camera for an end-of-season video called *Vintage G&T* which focused on the seasons of Marshall and his great friend Tony Lanfranchi. They provided the alcohol-fuelled commentary, and it remains one of the best productions of its kind, not only showcasing the 1986 Production Saloon Car season but also the thoughts of the two drivers and their acerbic observations on some of their rivals.

As the 1980s ended, Marshall had returned to racing TVRs in the new Tuscan Challenge and was busy in historic racing with a regular ride for Geoffrey Marsh in his collection of Aston Martins, one of which Gerry rescued from the bottom of a cliff after it had been used as a stunt car in a *Hammer House of Horror* film. There were outings in the Saab Turbo Championship, truck racing at Brands Hatch and Thundersaloons races in Nick Oatway's Pontiac V8-powered Opel Manta, the category an echo of the Super Saloons idea a decade before but with less freedom on modifications to curb costs. Then came the 1990s and 2000s and an increasing number of historic race outings in all manner of cars, with Marshall being a huge draw in the early days of the Goodwood Revival in which he excelled in anything he was offered to drive. Take the quirky Alvis Gray Lady, for example, which Ivan Dutton built for the 2004 Revival and in which Gerry wowed the crowd as it took on more conventional 1950s saloons.

The 1990s had been tough for Gerry Marshall. The sport was evolving, his DTV era was a memory

The 1990s had been tough for Gerry Marshall. The sport was evolving, his DTV era was a memory and his health was suffering as well.

and his health was suffering as well. There were operations for a hernia, prostate, hip and both knees and he was diagnosed in 2000 with polymyalgia rheumatica which made all his joints ache. Stoically, he did his own research, took his tablets and got on with life and was a regular in historic, rather than modern, racing paddocks. Indeed, on occasion he was reunited with some of his earlier cars, such as Baby Bertha which he relished as did the crowds who lined up to watch.

In 2005, he and his friend Colin Pearcy headed to Silverstone for a track day organised by the Historic Grand Prix Cars Association. Gerry went for a look and to find a car he could have a run in and sure enough there were willing owners. Marshall was on-track in a 1972 Chevrolet Camaro built by Roger Penske for Richard Petty, sideways out of Brooklands and Luffield before pulling off the track in front of the BRDC Clubhouse, having been

> Marshall was a man's man. Blokes loved his wit and irreverent attitude to life and his ability to tell stories, normally with a pint of beer and a cigar.

made a Life Member of the Club many years before. The first marshal on the scene assumed Gerry had run out of fuel, but the truth was far worse: he was dead. The cause of death was acute chronic myocardial ischaemia and severe coronary artery atherosclerosis, effectively blood flow to the heart being obstructed. Amazingly, Marshall had pulled the car to a stop safely and not only turned off the ignition but flicked off the fuel pumps as well. It was truly extraordinary as the car came sedately to a halt with no hint of the drama and tragedy within. British motor racing seemed to stop: Marshall, who had been a cornerstone of it for over four decades, was gone and for someone who attracted the limelight, it was done in such anonymous circumstances at a test day with few people around.

Marshall was a man's man. Blokes loved his wit and irreverent attitude to life and his ability to

tell stories, normally with a pint of beer and a cigar. He was opinionated and those opinions were unlikely to change, even with evidence. I remember discussing a now-deceased touring car driver and Gerry's opinion of him was: 'Wanker.' Ah, I pointed out, he had won two races recently. 'Lucky wanker.' The opinion wasn't to be changed. Indeed, Gerry could be a contradiction at times as he would go out of his way to help a friend, be it with advice or money, and yet as rival racer Norris Miles told Jeremy Walton for his Marshall biography: 'He got nasty sometimes with people who could help him and that didn't help his career.' Marshall's friends all agree, though, that if you needed someone on your side, it was Gerry. Indeed, such was his generosity that a few so-called friends often took advantage.

He was married three times and had girlfriends as well. He wasn't a model father, although that isn't to say that he didn't love his three children (Gregor, Justine and Tina) and as life slowed, he became a doting grandfather as his family grew. The children all reflected on how their relationships with him had their ups and downs, but in

An enduring image: Gerry Marshall outside the BRDC Clubhouse, pint in hand!

adulthood they could appreciate more what their father achieved, which was illustrated by the huge number of people who attended the celebration of his life in May 2005. It was standing room only . . .

Gerry Marshall was of his time. The modern age wouldn't have tolerated the drinking, smoking or some of the acerbic remarks, but in his pomp in the 1970s he *was* national racing. He was honoured for many seasons at Goodwood with an event in his name for saloon cars and the

Gerry Marshall Trophy is now a series of races for cars of his era.

Gerry Marshall will be remembered as a big man with a big heart who could drive anything and drive it hard. Out of the car he was a fan favourite and the fact that his memory lives on underlines just what an impact he had on motorsport. In 1978, he joined Jeremy Walton to write his first biography *Only Here for the Beer*, but there was so much more to Gerry Marshall than that. He was a true national racing hero.

James Hunt captured British interest in Formula 1 in the 1970s as he battled his way to the 1976 World Championship.

JAMES HUNT

Full name	James Simon Wallis Hunt
Birthdate	29 August 1947 (died 15 June 1993)
Place of birth	Belmont

Underneath the playboy image, James Hunt was
a fierce racing driver who carried a nation with
him to his world championship success.

James Hunt was the perfect racing driver for the 1970s. Handsome, well-spoken, fast, brave and a maverick character, he frustrated traditionalists and delighted his fans. He was a racing driver, had a string of attractive girlfriends and was in demand from the mainstream media as his lifestyle made him a commodity long before the advent of celebrity magazines. His Formula 1 career, certainly at the top, was relatively brief, but Hunt carved a career for himself as an outspoken commentator on the BBC's Formula 1 coverage until his sudden death in 1993. His season-battle with Niki Lauda in 1976 to win the Formula 1 World Championship was

immortalised in the movie *Rush* taking an extraordinary season in an extraordinary life to a new audience.

James Simon Wallis Hunt burst into the world in August 1947 and was described as a rebel from the very start. He was no academic, but at Wellington College he turned out to be an accomplished tennis player, representing the school and playing in the Junior Championships of Great Britain at Wimbledon, and musician as he performed one of Mozart's horn concertos for the crowds at an open-air school concert.

On Saturday 21 August 1965, James and his friend Christopher Ridge celebrated Hunt's 18th birthday by heading to Silverstone.

Hunt in a Hesketh. Silverstone, 1975, and James powers to fourth place in the Hesketh 308B-Cosworth in the British Grand Prix.

It was Hunt's first glimpse of motor racing and he was hooked. He had never heard of amateur racing, club racing as it is known, but found something that would satisfy his competitive instincts. He had been proficient at tennis, squash, cricket and golf but never considered a career in them, but motor racing invigorated him enough to rail against his parents' desire for him to become a doctor. His father, Wallis, realised James was fuelled by the idea of becoming a racing driver and funded lessons, at the cost of £165, at the Brands Hatch-based Jim Russell School. James was less than delighted: he felt that the lessons were beneath him, but Wallis had an ulterior motive which was that he hoped James would realise he wasn't good enough and drop the idea. Instead, James found a cheap Mini for sale in the pages of weekly newspaper *Motoring News* and was ready to race at Snetterton in Norfolk in the up to 1300cc class of a saloon car race in August 1967. However, the Mini was cheap for a reason and, without any windows, it failed scrutineering and Hunt was prevented from racing. Instead, it was October before he made his debut. There was nothing to suggest that a world champion was on the grid.

Hunt moved to the nascent Formula Ford 1600 category in 1968, the single-seater category launched the year before. The class was a huge success worldwide and produced many stars of the future, with Hunt showing his more sensible side by keeping out of trouble in his early races and garnering finishes, showing a maturity that would ebb away as he aged. By the summer of 1968, James Hunt was a race winner, the first coming at the Kent circuit of Lydden Hill in his Russell-Alexis Mk14, and while working at Telephone Rentals, he was becoming proficient at finding sponsorship. At the end of 1968, Hunt's progress had its first setback when he suffered a mighty accident at Oulton Park in Cheshire when he collected a spun Tony Dron. James was launched through an advertising hoarding and, in this pre-seatbelt era, was thrown from the car which submerged itself in the trackside lake. Next time out at Mallory Park, Hunt and Dron collided again, but in 1969 he was a regular race winner in his Merlyn Mk11A. He

was, however, starting to show an unpleasant side to his character, being rude to rookie journalist Ian Phillips (although Hunt later rang to apologise and the pair clicked) and when in Italy and told by the Vallelunga race organisers that his medical papers weren't in order and he couldn't race, Hunt parked his race car across the front of the grid and walked away. Ford's Head of Motorsport, Stuart Turner, who was sat in the grandstands was unimpressed but Mike Ticehurst who ran Motor Racing Enterprises was a fan and offered to run Hunt's car for him and let James concentrate on being a driver. By the end of 1969, James had moved up a rung and was racing Formula 3 cars, winning races but being involved in more than his share of accidents, earning the nickname 'Hunt the Shunt'.

And not only was James gaining a reputation as a crasher, but his arrogance and aggression was rearing its head more as well. Take Crystal Palace in October 1970, his home circuit in Central London and close to the 365 Club on King's Road in Chelsea in which James had spent a fair chunk of the week. In a race televised by the BBC, behind race leader Dave Walker was a massive battle for second place between Mike Beuttler, James and Dave Morgan. On the last lap, a desperate Morgan dived alongside Beuttler but made contact with James, their broken cars littering the pits straight within sight of the chequered flag. A furious Hunt leaped from his car, strode over to Morgan, all recorded by the BBC's cameras, and landed a solid blow, felling his rival before he strode away. The pair appeared at an RAC Tribunal at which Hunt escaped without penalty and Morgan was given a 12-month ban for dangerous driving. The pair had even appeared on BBC chat shows, starting the media's love affair with James.

James Hunt moved to McLaren in 1976 and although it was an uneasy fit at first, a world championship title followed.

Fast forward to 1972: James was about to embark on a fourth season in Formula 3 and was chosen to head the works March team, but the car proved to be a step back from the previous season's 713 model. James became disillusioned and publicly criticised the car and the team, before crashing the car at Silverstone in a race two weeks before the prestigious Monaco Grand Prix supporting event. Hunt wanted the works March team to sack him and pay him off but the team had no spare cash and wanted Hunt to walk away. A stand-off ensued but when Hunt's car arrived at Monaco it wasn't repaired from its Silverstone crash. James didn't think the sole mechanic, tired after driving from England, was going to be able to fix it in time and so elected to drive for his old team manager Chris Marshall instead. March, led by Max Mosley, warned Hunt not to drive as he would be in breach of his contract, but James ignored him and raced for Marshall, clattering into the Armco and damaging his suspension plus earning the sack from March. His career seemed to be washed up, but a chance meeting in a field at the Belgian Chimay circuit would change Hunt's life.

His career seemed to be washed up, but a chance meeting in a field at the Belgian Chimay circuit would change Hunt's life.

He bumped into Anthony 'Bubbles' Horsley, friend of petrolhead team owner Lord (Alexander) Hesketh. The team needed a driver, Hunt needed a drive: it started badly with yet more crashes for Hunt the Shunt, especially one at the British Grand Prix in which not only did James have a monster accident in the F3 race but contrived to destroy his road car in an accident leaving the circuit. That August, Hesketh decided to step up to Formula 2 taking James with him and his maiden race would be in the Brands Hatch Rothmans 50,000, the race's title in reference to the total prize fund. The race catered for F1, F2 and Formula 5000 cars and James finished second in the F2 class. It seemed his career had been revived and hence the team entered 1973 in high hopes. They were quickly dashed . . . The team bought a Surtees TS15 from motorcycle-turned-F1 world champion John Surtees but it wasn't

Hunt took pole for the opening race in Brazil but crashed out when the throttle stuck open but was second in South Africa.

a good car and Hunt struggled as Hesketh saw his expenditure outweigh his return. And then he had a brainwave. For the money he was spending to be at the back of a Formula 2 grid, he could spend roughly the same to be at the back of an F1 grid. And so James Hunt became a Formula 1 driver.

Hesketh abandoned his F2 season in May 1973 and Hunt was aboard a March 731 for the Monaco Grand Prix that same month. That James was classified ninth, despite a late engine drama forcing him to park, was an amazing result. Better was to come as 'Young Master James' took third in the Dutch Grand Prix and then second to Ronnie Peterson's Lotus 72 in the season-closer at Watkins Glen in America. For 1974, Hesketh continued with March but only for the first five races before its own chassis hit the track, with which Hunt took three podium finishes and then a popular win at Zandvoort on his

birthday in 1975, his reputation enhanced by sports car drives and Formula 5000 in America.

But just when it seemed that Hunt was on the crest of the wave, it all came crashing down. Hesketh could no longer justify the expense of being an unsponsored, independent F1 team and it seemed that James was out of a drive. Fate again intervened as McLaren's lead driver, the 1972 and 1974 world champion Emerson Fittipaldi, was off to drive for his family's Copersucar-backed F1 project. McLaren needed a driver; Hunt needed a drive. Although team principal Teddy Mayer wasn't convinced, Marlboro's John Hogan was a Hunt fan and convinced Mayer to recruit him for 1976 which turned out to be one of those seasons that lives in the memory with drama, controversy and Niki Lauda's near-life-ending accident, all used as the basis for Ron Howard's *Rush* movie.

Hunt for McLaren versus Austrian Lauda at Ferrari. Hunt took pole for the opening race in Brazil but crashed out when the throttle stuck open but was second in South Africa. He crashed with Frenchman Patrick Depillar at Long Beach. He won in Spain but the McLaren was protested by Ferrari in the first

James carried the coveted number 1 on his McLaren M23-Cosworth in 1977. At the non-championship Race of Champions at Brands Hatch, he won by 23 seconds.

signs of the acrimony that would be an undercurrent to the season, the Italian *Scuderia*'s contention being that the car was too wide. With a new Goodyear radial tyre, rather than its old cross-ply, there was a bulge to the tyre instead of a flat sidewall. That meant the car was wider than the regulations by 1.8 mm. Hunt was disqualified, although would later be reinstated on appeal.

He won in France and then came the British Grand Prix held at Brands Hatch which was packed to the rafters to cheer on Britain's home-grown hero. A first corner clash between Ferrari teammates Lauda and Clay Regazzoni resulted

in 'Regga' spinning and Hunt being left with nowhere to go. He hit Regazzoni, was launched onto two wheels and crashed back to terra firma damaging his suspension, but Jacques Laffite's Ligier had been caught up in the mêlée and the race was stopped as Hunt tried to assess the damage to the McLaren. He had hurt his thumb, but the car had greater damage, meaning that he needed to use the spare car if it were allowed. Discussions lasted for over 40 minutes as a restless crowd started to vent its anger. The fans wanted to see Hunt in the race and eventually officials relented and allowed Hunt to race the spare car,

Amidst the drama of the 1976 British Grand Prix, it is easy to forget that James won a year later at Silverstone and from pole, too. Marshals and media alike wanted to talk to him.

in which James won the race and was promptly protested by Ferrari. This time there was no reprieve: the disqualification stood although given the length of the delay, it is possible that McLaren could have repaired the original car after all.

Hunt looked to be out of the championship fight but fate again intervened when Niki Lauda had a massive accident in the German Grand Prix at the imposing Nürburgring circuit. Lauda was

pulled from his burning car and taken to hospital where he was read the last rites. There was little hope of him surviving so the fact that he missed just two races was miraculous. He returned, bandaged, at Monza for the Italian Grand Prix where he finished amazingly at fourth and the championship battle went to the last race in Japan. Again, in a season of drama, the start was delayed as the torrential rain showed little sign of relenting but when it did, Lauda soon retired as he wasn't prepared to risk his life again, needlessly. But the story wasn't done yet, as Hunt had to pit with a puncture and with confusion as to the race order, didn't realise he was champion. Post-race footage showed an irate Hunt remonstrating with Mayer until he was calmed enough to listen to the news: he was third and world champion.

After two more frustrating seasons at McLaren, he moved to Wolf for 1979 but quit after seven races never to return. Instead, he moved into broadcasting where he formed a hugely successful partnership with Murray Walker, his acerbic and pithy comments winning him many fans.

Hunt was known as a womaniser, a drinker and a smoker. His marriage to Suzy Miller ended in divorce and she later married actor Richard Burton, before a long-term relationship with Jane Birbeck had to endure the pain of a miscarriage. He married Sarah Lomax who bore him two sons, Tom and Freddie, and he was planning on marrying girlfriend Helen Dyson before his death. Hunt's promiscuity is no secret and well-documented, although amazingly there are few, if any, kiss-and-tell stories and no known illegitimate children. One

of his favourite clincher-lines in a chat-up was to tell a reluctant girl, 'But I might be killed in the race.' Bubbles Horsley once overheard this and said to James when in his car: 'Killed in the race? You'd better go a bit quicker then.'

His early BBC commentaries became legend when, scruffily dressed and often barefoot, he would arrive with a bottle of wine, but it would be wrong to suggest

By the end of 1978, James was ready to leave McLaren, but his move to Wolf wasn't a success. He walked away from F1 midway through 1979.

that he was feckless. Indeed, he was one of the first drivers on the scene of Ronnie Peterson's fatal accident at Monza in 1978 and was able to drag Peterson from his wrecked car. The press hailed him as a hero, which annoyed James greatly after a difficult season in which the media had knocked him at every opportunity. 'When you are down they kick you and then they kick you again,' he said. 'When you are up, they go right over the top.'

Hunt blamed Riccardo Patrese for the accident and held the grudge long into his commentating career, criticising him at any opportunity and perhaps this was one of his failings, although some viewers loved it: James had strong opinions. Of triple world champion Nelson Piquet, he said on air: '(What) I can't understand is why he doesn't drive faster, just out of self-respect.' Mauricio Gugelmin earned: 'He was slow in all the lesser formulae, even slower in Formula 1.' And ragged Italian Andrea de Cesaris, who had a reputation as a crasher much like Hunt in his youth, was described as an 'embarrassment to himself, his team and the sport'. BBC producers cringed, but viewers lapped it up.

By 1993, James Hunt seemed to be a different character. He was healthier than ever, had quit smoking and drinking and his life was back on track. He was taking his BBC role more seriously than ever and had a syndicated newspaper column in the *Daily Telegraph* but a costly divorce from Sarah Lomax had decimated his fortune. Living in Wimbledon in a house he owned but on just £500 a week, James sought work wherever he could find it. In 1993, the BBC's Canadian Grand Prix commentary would be remote from a studio in London. James cycled there and back. The following day, he wrote his newspaper column, spoke to Helen Dyson who was holidaying in Greece and proposed to her over the phone. Then, he invited his male friends around, cooked dinner and played snooker. Eventually it was time to turn in. James Hunt climbed the stairs in his Wimbledon home, but before he made it to his bed, he suffered a massive heart attack and died. He was found by close friend Mike Dennett the following day.

The impact was huge. A void was left in the sport and broadcasting with the ultimate irony being that a man who had lived – and partied – hard should die when he had taken the time and trouble to

James Hunt's F1 career was relatively brief but it netted a World Championship and 10 wins.

straighten out his life emotionally, physically and financially.

James Hunt won only one motor racing championship in his career, the 1976 Formula 1 World Championship, one well-documented in print as well as on screen. He won 10 grands prix and his time in the highest echelon lasted just five full seasons although it straddled seven in all. That James was cited by future world champion Kimi Räikkönen as his hero was telling, Räikkönen even using the moniker James Hunt under which to compete in a snowmobile race. The Finn was 13 when Hunt died.

Who knows what Hunt would have made of the following eras of Formula 1, of DRS and of some of the drivers now involved with their political and social views all aired on social media. What is certain is that that wonderful voice, those trenchant views and combative drives will remain with anyone who watched him race or listened to him commentate. Racing driver, playboy, free spirit, broadcaster, enthusiast and father: there are so many tags that can be associated with James Hunt who was and remains one of British motor racing's most memorable figures.

Nigel Mansell celebrates his 1987 British Grand Prix win at Silverstone.

Full name	Nigel Ernest James Mansell
Birthdate	8 August 1953
Place of birth	Upton upon Severn

One of the bravest men ever to step into a
racing car, Nigel Mansell excelled in winning
the 1992 title but never defended his crown.

Lap 64 of the 1986 Australian Grand Prix was pure Nigel Mansell. Running in second place and hunting for a maiden Formula 1 world title, Mansell's left-rear Goodyear tyre exploded. In an instant, there was the loss of the championship, the drama as the rubber flailed, sparks flew and the car twitched and the gaining of many new fans as the underdog shone through. Mansell lost and won in different respects.

Nigel Mansell's motor racing career was never dull and he was just what Fleet Street wanted. He was always good for a story, always at the centre of drama and yet while he could work his magic in a racing car, there was a side to him that came across as a whinger,

a drama queen, never able to admit that things were his fault. But that shouldn't take anything away from his bravery in a car and his commitment out of it.

Right from the start of Nigel Ernest James Mansell's motor racing career there was drama. He began, like so many, in the hard-knock school of karting and contrived to roll on the warming-up lap of his first race. It set the tone for a remarkable career. That karting drama behind him, Mansell soon joined the British Junior Team and qualified for the World Championship Finals in 1969 in Milan where he bagged third. Car racing came in 1976 when Mansell moved to Formula Ford 1600 in a Hawke DL11. He

Nigel's Lotus 95T-Renault retired from the 1984 British Grand Prix after 24 laps with a gearbox problem.

made his debut at Mallory Park and won five of his season's 11 races. Onlookers were impressed. His first title came in 1977 when he began the season with a Javelin chassis but it was outpaced and he switched to a Crosse 25F and then the newer 32F. History records that he won the Brush Fusegear FF1600 Championship from South African Trevor van Rooyen but ignores one important aspect of the season: a collision first time out in the 32F put him hard into the banking at

Brands Hatch and left Nigel with a broken neck and a crushed vertebra. Having given up his job as a Lucas Aerospace engineer three weeks before, he knew he couldn't take the doctor's advice of being laid up for six weeks for fear of going broke. Instead, Nigel discharged himself and went on to win that title.

Formula 3 beckoned but offers were limited and Mansell's budget prevented him from paying for more than four races in 1978. For 1979, though, he was on the grid for a full season in a Unipart-sponsored March 793 with its Triumph Dolomite engine. A win came early in the season, but the nadir was at Oulton Park in September when Italian Andrea de Cesaris cannoned into Mansell and flipped him upside down. It did more damage to Nigel's back and left him in bed, penniless. And then the phone rang . . .

Lotus wanted him to test its Formula 1 car and in true Mansell fashion, Nigel agreed. He wasn't going to tell the team he was injured, so he armed himself with painkillers and headed to Paul Ricard in France. Four weeks later, he committed his signature to a testing contract. See what I mean about commitment? Another example came in 1980 when he was offered his first grand prix race. It would be in Austria and Nigel lined up 24th and last. On the grid, Lotus mechanics topped up the fuel burned having driven to the grid, but they contrived to slosh some into the cockpit and after a handful of laps it had seeped through Mansell's overalls. He was in severe pain, but what was a grand prix rookie to do? Mansell's answer was to continue. Engine failure on lap 41 brought merciful relief and

medical treatment was required, but he had done enough to earn more drives that season.

His Lotus career continued as the team struggled for results and then lost its leader, Colin Chapman, in 1982. Chapman had been a great supporter of Mansell and knew how to deal with his ego, a skill that his successors didn't possess. By 1984, still without a win, Mansell was coping with a frosty relationship with team manager Peter Warr but led a grand prix for the first time. On the streets of Monaco, a venue he loved, Mansell's Lotus-Renault was pulling away from the pack, but on a treacherous surface, rather than reducing his pace he went faster. Suddenly, heading up the hill through Beau Rivage, the car got away from him and he cannoned into the Armco. Rather than admit he had made a mistake, he blamed the white painted road markings and that was the start of an uneasy relationship between

He wasn't going to tell the team he was injured, so he armed himself with painkillers and headed to Paul Ricard in France.

Mansell and the media. It also affected Mansell's self-confidence, especially when Peter Warr publicly stated that: 'Nigel Mansell will never win a grand prix as long as I have a hole in my arse.'

For 1985, Mansell switched to Williams where he was guided by team manager Peter Collins, a self-confessed Mansell fan. He was able to get the moustachioed Brummie to concentrate more on his driving and less on what people were saying (and printing) and Mansell started to believe in himself once more. In October, there was a second grand prix in Britain, run under the Grand Prix of Europe title. Mansell was running second and closing on Ayrton Senna's Lotus when they came upon Mansell's teammate Keke Rosberg heading for the pit lane. Senna hesitated and Mansell swept by into a lead he was never to lose. Finally! He'd

made it! A win in the next race in South Africa proved that Brands Hatch had been no fluke.

As wins came in 1986, at Spa-Francorchamps, Montreal, Paul Ricard, Brands Hatch and Estoril, it looked as though a championship was a real possibility. Pressure perhaps got to him in the penultimate race in Mexico when he didn't put the car in gear on the start line and he salvaged fifth. That left Australia and he was running second, when even third would have sufficed. Bang! The exploded tyre took his dream of the title with it. A year later, Mansell was in contention for the championship again, this time fighting with teammate Nelson Piquet with whom he had a frosty relationship. He crashed spectacularly in qualifying for the last race in Japan and this time there was no grin-and-bear-it attitude: he withdrew from the race and publicly aired his pain. The following season was a lean one as Williams lost its Honda engine supply and for 1989 he was wearing red, now a Ferrari driver. A win first time out in Brazil made sure the relationship started well, but perhaps inevitably it soured, as in 1990 he was joined by Alain Prost, by now a three-time world champion. As Prost made the team

> As wins came in 1986, at Spa-Francorchamps, Montreal, Paul Ricard, Brands Hatch and Estoril, it looked as though a championship was a real possibility.

Mansell won a restarted British Grand Prix, the last to be held at Brands Hatch, in 1986 as his rivalry with teammate Nelson Piquet increased.

work around him, Mansell's need for support showed and that, coupled with mechanical woes, led to a theatrical exit from the British Grand Prix when, having parked his car at Copse Corner with engine failure, he threw his gloves to the crowd and announced his retirement. The press lapped it up, although behind the scenes, Mansell was being courted by Williams and he was on the grid for his old team in 1991. Five wins came, one crucially at Silverstone as he won on home soil, and for 1992 the Williams brains-trust of Patrick Head and Adrian Newey gave Mansell his best shot at the championship with

the outstanding Renault-engined FW14B chassis. With active ride suspension, an excellent engine and a team on the crest of a wave, Our Nige won nine races including Silverstone again at which Mansell Mania was at such a height, whipped up by the media, that many fans invaded the track to celebrate almost as soon as Mansell took the chequered flag. And yet, and yet . . .

His relationship with Williams had sunk to a new low and team owner Frank Williams, never one to exude much sympathy over drivers, was looking elsewhere during the season. He signed Damon Hill and

Bang! An exploded tyre in Adelaide cost Mansell a chance to win the 1986 World Championship.

Alain Prost for 1993 leaving the new world champion with limited options. Mansell could have opted for a different, lesser team on the grid but that was not his style. Instead, he stormed off to America to race – and win – in IndyCar, America's home-grown and popular single-seater series. He won from pole first time out at Surfers Paradise and oh-so-nearly won the Indy 500 before being outfoxed by Emerson Fittipaldi after a late-race caution. He took the title and returned to the UK at the end of the season to drive in the non-championship TOCA Shoot-Out, a race for two-litre touring cars, most from the successful British Touring Car Championship. It was promoter Robert Fearnall who had the idea of approaching Mansell and he agreed, but his

touring car outing came to a metal-grinding end coming out of the Old Hairpin. Sideways, he fought his Ford Mondeo and as he did so was clipped by the following Tiff Needell (Vauxhall Cavalier). Mansell was sent left into the wall in front of Starkey's Bridge, the wrecked Mondeo spinning into retirement. The race was stopped and it was a long time before Mansell was extricated from the car. To this day accounts from those present differ as to whether he was unconscious or milking the situation for all it was worth. Either way, it added to the Mansell legend but Fearnall's 60,000-strong crowd had more than paid for Mansell's appearance fee and Ford had huge publicity from the race, for all manner of reasons!

Five years later, Mansell was back on a touring car grid, again for Ford as he attacked selected races in 1998. His IndyCar career had ended after an uncompetitive 1994 and he had even returned to Williams after the death of Ayrton Senna to win a 31st grand prix in Australia. Plans were made for him to join McLaren for 1995 but he retired after just two races largely because he couldn't fit comfortably in the car. It was a sad end to a Formula 1 career that had delivered so much excitement for a decade and a half. He, and his fans, expected much, but the British Touring Car Championship was at its zenith with outstanding teams, engineers and drivers on the grid. Whatever he believed, Mansell wasn't in for an easy time. He was only entered for three events, so six races, thus putting him at a disadvantage and fifth place was his best result at a wet Donington in a race that he came close to winning, but the regulars had other ideas: John Cleland came out on

A move to Ferrari came in 1989. Nigel won the first race in Brazil and, here, finished second at Silverstone that summer.

Williams was the team that gave Mansell his first win and his sole World Championship in 1992.

top. Another break came before he returned in the Grand Prix Masters concept for F1 veterans and won two races as his sons, Greg and Leo, started their careers. In 2010, they teamed up in sports car racing and Nigel joined racer and ice cream magnate Andrew Howard to form Beechdean Mansell Motorsport to race at Le Mans. A puncture caused Nigel to crash out early, Mansell saying that the impact left him so concussed that he was unable to recognise his family and in order to get his brain to work again, took up magic. Mansell is now a member of the magic circle.

That he threw himself into the discipline was no surprise. Whatever Mansell tried, he brought that amazing commitment and determination to it. He became a very proficient golfer, playing in the 1988 Australian Open thanks to his friendship with Greg Norman and also won the World Senior Championship twice and his love of golf resulted in him owning courses in the UK and then America. Equally, when living on the Isle of Man, he threw himself into local life by becoming a Special Constable on the island's police force, happy to put something back into a place which welcomed him with open arms.

If Mansell had his detractors in the press corps, they took him to new heights in the public's affections and, let's face it, he delivered good copy along the way. The public loved his determination in the searing heat of Dallas in 1984, where he had scored his first career pole position when he pushed his ailing Lotus to the line, its gearbox broken as he tried to salvage sixth place. He gained a championship point and then collapsed next to the car. It was that kind of determination, with an element of theatre, that won him fans. It was the same with the puncture in Australia: it didn't just deflate, it *exploded*. In Japan in 1987 when he crashed in practice, the car became *airborne* as it spun from the tyre barrier, and in 1986 when he won at Brands Hatch in the spare car which was designed for teammate Piquet, he was so dehydrated that he had to be held upright on the podium. In Austria in 1987, he arrived fresh from having his wisdom teeth extracted. They were in a bag and an ice pack was held to his jaw and yet he won the race. On the way to the podium in an open vehicle, he stood up too soon and

whacked his head on a metal girder overhead. It could have been nasty, but he brushed it off although he was savvy enough to know that Fleet Street was making a story out of it.

On one memorable occasion, though, the Mansell theatre bit and it bit hard. Canada, 1991. Mansell had qualified second and was dominating the race by over a minute when he came into the final hairpin. There, Nigel decided to wave to his fans and as he did so the car cut out. People claimed he had stalled but Mansell denied this, Williams saying that it was an electrical fault. True, but it was induced by Mansell who was so busy waving that he let the revs drop and there wasn't enough power to charge the electrical and hydraulic systems, thus causing the gearbox barrel to become stuck. When the car was returned to the pits, the engine was refired and the gearbox worked perfectly, but as ever Mansell wasn't one to accept a mistake nor eat humble pie: instead, it was someone else's fault, be it the team's, the car's, the gearbox's . . . The team did take responsibility, principally team manager Peter Windsor, when in Estoril that same season, the car was allowed away without

Ford used the Mansell magic for promotional purposes when it entered him in selected British Touring Car Championship races in 1998. He led at Donington but lost out to John Cleland's Vauxhall Vectra.

a rear wheel tightened. The car shed the unfastened wheel and stopped in the fast lane of the pits where a new wheel was attached. The stewards excluded him for having a wheel changed outside the car's pit box. Again, drama.

On occasions, perhaps Nigel was naïve. He knew the fans loved him and assumed that so did everyone else. He was outmanoeuvred politically at Ferrari by Prost and butted heads with Piquet at Williams, Nelson referring to Mansell as 'An uneducated blockhead'. He assumed, understandably, that as hot property in 1992 a continuation of his contract would

be a formality, but he hadn't seen the threat of a political Prost coming up to challenge him, nor an acceptance of the deteriorating relationship between him, Frank Williams and Patrick Head.

But for the many thousands of Mansell fans, they shared his disappointments with him and celebrated his successes as well. That Silverstone in 1992 was so busy was largely down to Mansell, especially as he was the favourite to win after an impressive start to the season. Those fans who loved him as the underdog and voted him BBC Sports Personality of the Year in 1986 after his defeat in Adelaide now cheered him to the echo. It was no surprise, therefore, that they didn't share Frank Williams' decision to replace Mansell for 1993 and, with more than a little encouragement from *The Sun* newspaper, protested outside the Williams factory with their 'Save Our Nigel' banners. It was pointless, of course, although Mansell would be back for a handful of races in 1994 orchestrated by F1 ringmaster Bernie Ecclestone who knew the sport needed a big name on the grid after the death of Ayrton Senna.

A year after winning the Formula 1 World Championship, Nigel was winning Stateside. In the CART Indy Car World Series, Mansell attacks the Corkscrew at Laguna Seca on his way to winning the title.

At a time when British sport, and motor racing in particular, needed a hero, Nigel Mansell fitted the bill perfectly. When he won, he won in style. When he lost, he lost dramatically. He always drove bravely.

Mansell, with help from Williams and its PR consultancy CSS Promotions, also made something out of his race number, long before drivers were able to choose a number and exploit it as a brand. Initially a means of identifying Mansell's Williams from his teammate's, the number 5 on the car's nosecone was painted red, and that became part of the Mansell mystique: Red 5 became part of him on those seasons that he drove for Williams. For six seasons, Red 5 was Mansell, a nod to the Red Arrows, that very British institution.

Wherever you saw that familiar number, however, you knew, just knew, something was going to happen. Mansell was never one to settle for position. Take Monaco in 1992 when he lost the lead to Ayrton Senna's McLaren after pitting for

tyres. Mansell crawled all over the back of the Brazilian for lap after lap, never finding a gap but never once giving up. And, of course, as he darted left and right, harrying his rival, the fans loved him for it.

Mansell continued as an FIA Formula 1 steward, never camera shy, and remains one of the greatest British drivers the sport has witnessed. The most naturally gifted? No. One of the bravest? Certainly. One of the most determined? Undoubtedly. At a time when British sport, and motor racing in particular, needed a hero, Nigel Mansell fitted the bill perfectly. When he won, he won in style. When he lost, he lost dramatically. He always drove bravely. He put the sport on the front pages of the newspapers as well as the back and he brought many new fans to the sport. The sadness is that we never saw him defend his world championship in 1993: it wouldn't have been easy perhaps, but it would have been fascinating. A single world crown sells short a Great Briton.

BRANDS HATCH
FORMULA ONE WORLD CHAM

Shell Oils · Shell Oils · Shell Oils · Shell

An exhausted Nigel Mansell after winning the 1986 British Grand Prix at Brands Hatch.

A second place in the 1994 Monaco Grand Prix was an excellent result for Martin Brundle, especially as his McLaren MP4/9 was powered by the oft-unreliable Peugeot engine.

MARTIN BRUNDLE

Full name	Martin John Brundle
Birthdate	1 June 1959
Place of birth	King's Lynn

Martin Brundle is an accomplished driver
and an outstanding broadcaster whose
knowledge and style have won many fans.

To a whole generation of motor racing fans, especially Formula 1, Martin Brundle is known as an outstanding broadcaster, one with opinions and an excellent ability to translate the technicalities of the sport to the layman. He has never been one to hark back to his day, the good old days, but instead embraces every season as the best yet. Part of that is a broadcaster's duty, true, but in Brundle's case it is because he genuinely loves the sport and remains excited by the people and the cars that sustain it. Not only that, but he has put something back into the sport with an essential role in protecting the future of the British Grand Prix while chairman of the British Racing Drivers' Club.

Oddly, for someone so inextricably linked to Formula 1, it was a category that wasn't especially kind to him. His best finishes were second places at Monza in 1992 and Monaco in 1994 and for much of his career in F1, Martin was saddled with an uncompetitive car or a faster teammate. Or both . . . Therefore, it is in sports car racing that he achieved his best results: Le Mans and Daytona 24 Hours winner and World Sports Car Champion.

Martin John Brundle had an unorthodox path to Formula 1 and had a career which, like many of our Immortals, included different disciplines. As a 12-year-old, Martin started grasstrack racing in a Ford Anglia and then spread his wings to local Hot Rod

Audi badge on his overalls, Martin Brundle raced for the German brand in the 1980 and 1981 British Saloon Car Championship seasons.

racing in East Anglia moving to the red grade, for the most successful drivers, by the end of 1976. As the year concluded, he abandoned his Ford Escort for a Toyota Celica and went circuit racing, trying Special Saloon racing (for highly modified saloon cars) towards the end of the year.

As the family business was a Toyota dealership, it made sense

for Brundle, who tended to go under the tag of Marty in his youth, to campaign a Celica in the British Saloon Car Championship for 1977, the Toyota a competitive proposition in the under 1600cc class of the category. A win came at Silverstone and Martin stayed on for a second season in which he went winless but took seventh overall. For 1979, Brundle switched disciplines, trying his hand at single-seater racing by moving into Formula Ford 2000, a category for single-seater cars with 2-litre Ford engines. He won at Snetterton in Norfolk, his home circuit, and continued in saloon cars by having outings in the British championship plus he graced the grids of the new BMW County Championship, for dealer-entered identical BMW 323i models. This was down to the man behind the series, Tom Walkinshaw, who was also running successful saloon car teams at the time. Martin later described Walkinshaw as: 'The man I owe most of my racing career to. (I) Wrote Tom a letter as a teenager and he gave me a chance and I seized the opportunity.' He won at Donington Park and was firmly on Walkinshaw's radar, especially after two more BMW County Championship wins in 1980 alongside more FF2000 outings.

In 1981, Walkinshaw had three manufacturer programmes on the go for the British Saloon Car Championship, entrusted to run the Rover 3500, Mazda RX-7 and Audi 80 programmes. He took over the Audi programme from Richard Lloyd and with it came one of its drivers, Stirling Moss.

Stirling had endured a tricky 1980 season and Walkinshaw knew that he needed results as well as the PR value, so Brundle was installed in the second car and took two class wins. By the end of the season, he was back in a single-seater making his Formula 3 debut at Thruxton and finished fourth in the 1982 British F3 Championship for Dave Price Racing. It made him one of the favourites for the

In 1983, Martin took the fight to Ayrton Senna in the Marlboro British Formula 3 Championship. His first win came at Silverstone in round 10 of the 20.

Brundle made his Formula 1 debut in 1984 with Tyrrell. Although the team lost its points for a regulation breach, Martin impressed on his debut in Brazil to finish fifth on the road.

1983 season as he switched to Eddie Jordan's team. Except . . .

In one of those unfortunate pieces of timing that seemed to hover over Brundle's career, he found himself on the same grid as Ayrton Senna who had wowed everyone with his pace and prowess in Formula Ford 1600 and then FF2000 over the previous two seasons. Brundle knew he was in for a fight. Senna won the first nine races, enough to break anyone's resolve, but Brundle never gave up and after Senna crashed out of round 10 at Silverstone, Brundle took a win and had his confidence boosted. The season came alive, as did their rivalry, such as a race at Oulton Park where a quicker-starting Brundle headed Senna until Ayrton launched a move up the inside, rode over Brundle's wheels and landed atop Brundle's Ralt RT3. Senna won the championship eventually, Brundle taking second as well as a win for Walkinshaw in the European Touring Car Championship's wet Donington three-hour race and the F3 race supporting the Austrian

Grand Prix. A move to F1 beckoned for 1984 as Martin headed for underdog British team Tyrrell and Senna headed to another British underdog, Toleman. Martin was fifth on his debut in Brazil but suffered a sizeable accident in qualifying in Monaco, his wrecked car ending on its side. He took an outstanding second in Detroit, but a season-ending crash was to come in Dallas when he hit the wall in qualifying and badly broke both his ankles. He was out for the rest of the season, although his comeback race was a grand prix of sorts . . . the first ever British Truck Grand Prix when he drove a Renault at Donington. As if the injuries weren't enough to put the dampers on his season, Tyrrell was then found guilty of fuel tank irregularities that meant all of the team's results were scrubbed from the record books.

A second season for Tyrrell followed in 1985 in a normally aspirated car against an increasing number of turbocharged rivals meaning results were hard to come by. He got his hands on a turbocharged chassis mid-season, but in the days when only the top six were afforded points, his best of seventh gave no reward. He stayed with Tyrrell for '86 and his Renault turbo-engined car garnered fifth in Brazil and at Brands Hatch, sixth in Hungary and he ended the season on a high with fourth in Australia. Frustration with Tyrrell prompted a move to the German Zakspeed team for 1987, but this proved to be a mistake as only once did Martin finish in the points, fifth in San Marino, but 10 retirements and two races in which he was so far back he wasn't classified added to his unhappiness.

Throughout this period in F1, Martin had continued to drive for Walkinshaw. He had raced his Jaguar XJ-S in the 1984 European Touring Car Championship and went with Tom to sports car racing as Walkinshaw's TWR operation took over the Jaguar operation in Group C racing in 1985. Indeed, it was sports car racing that was giving Martin the success he craved, and in 1987 he was part of the winning crew in the 1000-kilometre races at Brands

Martin was fifth on his debut in Brazil but suffered a sizeable accident in qualifying in Monaco, his wrecked car ending on its side.

Hatch and Spa-Francorchamps. So, Brundle's reasoning was that he could win with TWR and Jaguar or be at the back in F1. He elected to walk away from Formula 1 for 1988 and concentrated on sports cars, winning the season-starting Daytona 24 Hours with Raul Boesel and John Nielsen and he won the World Sports Car Championship after wins at Jarama, Monza, Silverstone, Brands Hatch and Fuji. Indeed, such was his reputation after such a season that Williams came knocking when it needed someone to sub for a chicken-pox-infected Nigel Mansell for the Belgian Grand Prix. Martin took ninth having worked his tyres a bit too hard early on, but his pace reminded people in the paddock of his ability. Thus, he was back on the grid for 1989 at Brabham and although the once-great team now had to pre-qualify for races, Martin still took sixth at Monaco, but with little guarantee of budget nor development, Martin bailed for 1990 and went back to sports cars instead. He was back in a Jaguar. Winning the Le Mans 24 Hours, with Nielsen and Price Cobb was the highlight, but there were wins in the American-based IMSA series as well and he also took a win on his way to third in the championship in the

American-based IROC (International Race of Champions) series. Surrounded by American racing legends, a race win for a European was quite a feat, and his third in the standings netted him $50,000.

The promise of a new Yamaha engine tempted Martin back to Brabham for 1991 but a fifth place in Japan aside, it was another disappointing year as the reliability of the car was poor and development was limited. In sports cars, though, Martin took third in the British Empire Trophy at Silverstone, a drive that he recalled as the race of his life. His Jaguar XJR-14 suffered a 10-minute delay early on when the throttle cable broke and Martin crawled into the pit lane. As mechanics went to work, team boss Tom Walkinshaw quickly switched Martin's co-driver Derek Warwick to the second car to share with Teo Fabi, in an effort to score points. Eventually, Brundle was sent back into the race and he flew, attacking the old airfield circuit for all he was worth. Ultimately, with Warwick now in the sister car, he drove the entire race, all two hours and 12 minutes, on his own and was in tears of exhaustion at the end. He was without a drink bottle as he expected to only do

Having forged a successful partnership with Tom Walkinshaw, Martin won in Jaguars in touring cars and in Group C sports car racing.

a 45-minute stint before handing over to Warwick. Instead, he was in the car, flat out, for the whole race. He finished third, four laps down after the earlier delays and while it was gruelling, it was another example of Brundle's resilience and ability.

For 1992 Martin was in a good team, a good car and with someone he knew well overseeing it all: Tom Walkinshaw was joint team principal at Benetton and recruited Brundle to join the team. It was make-or-break for Martin, rescued really by Walkinshaw, but

timing was against him. Just as he joined a front-running team, he found German *wünderkind* Michael Schumacher on the other side of the garage in his first full F1 season. Schumacher's raw speed, especially in qualifying, came as a shock to Brundle and the start of his season, which involved three accidents in the first four races, badly dented his confidence. Worse, the Benetton team lost confidence as well and although Martin regrouped to score points in the last nine races and came close to winning the

An airborne Brundle starts his frightening roll in Melbourne at the start of the 1996 Australian Grand Prix.

Canadian Grand Prix before a rare mechanical failure, he was shown the door at the end of the year.

A year later, Brundle was in blue as he raced for the French Ligier team and netted a podium in San Marino on his way to seventh in the championship. Rather than stay on, Martin jumped to McLaren for 1994, grabbing the seat vacated by long-time rival Senna. Again, timing was against Brundle as this was the year that Ron Dennis' team formed an alliance with Peugeot as its engine partner. The French engines were fragile at best and Brundle's season was summed up at Silverstone when, having qualified ninth, the lights changed, he let out the clutch and the engine let go in a sheet of flame. That he took second in Monaco was somewhat miraculous given that the race was 78 laps long . . .

Brundle was keen to stay on and help the team move forward for 1995 but timing, politics as well, was significant again. Nigel Mansell, back after his spell in America, was on the market and McLaren wanted a star name so the 1992 world champion was duly signed for what turned out to be a disastrous two-race campaign as he wouldn't fit the car properly. Brundle, pondering what might

For 1996 Martin was reunited with his old F3 team boss Eddie Jordan and the pressure was on the team to deliver the goods.

have been, moved back to Ligier for a part season in which the team had three drivers for two seats: engine provider Mugen-Honda insisted on Japanese driver Aguri Suzuki for some of the races so he and Brundle had to share the car, although Martin took a third at Spa.

For 1996 Martin was reunited with his old F3 team boss Eddie Jordan and the pressure was on the team to deliver the goods. Martin's season started badly, having qualified on the back row of the grid, with a huge crash on the opening lap of the Australian Grand Prix, his Jordan 196 rolling at the start of the race. He was able to take the spare car for the restart and started from the pit lane, but by his own admission had forgotten that the lack of a warming-up lap would mean the brakes were cold. Thus, he had only himself to blame when he collided with Pedro Diniz's Ligier on the opening lap of the restart.

A fourth place was his best finish but finally he accepted that the drives weren't there anymore and his F1 career was over.

Sadly, despite Jordan now having healthy backing from Benson & Hedges cigarettes, there was dissent internally as the team still failed to make the necessary step forward and the car itself was lacking grip. Yet again, poor Brundle had found himself in the wrong place at the wrong time. A fourth place was his best finish but finally he accepted that the drives weren't there anymore and his F1 career was over. F1 *driving* career, that is.

While suffering his job-share season at Ligier, Martin had found gainful employment in the BBC television commentary box. ITV took over the UK's Formula 1 coverage in 1997 and Brundle was the natural choice for the analyst's role, one which he took to instantly and was able to dovetail it with occasional races. Martin continued to race at Le Mans, for Nissan and then Toyota, then Bentley in 2001, although none of his forays replicated his 1990 success.

The competitive instinct never went away, though. Whenever possible, Brundle would find an angle for television to allow him to drive that season's F1 cars and guest drives abounded: he had a go in Formula Palmer Audi to race against his son, Alex; Lamborghini offered him a Super Trofeo one-make drive in 2010; Volkswagen offered him (and other retired F1 Brits) an outing in the Scirocco Cup and he raced a Radical too. He drove in the Daytona 24 Hours in 2011, in the Le Mans 24 Hours in 2012 (sharing a car with Alex) and in 2016 finished second in the sports car race supporting the Le Mans 24 Hours despite medical dramas just weeks before. Oh, and he was a regular at Goodwood in historic races. Brundle still loved racing and competing kept him sharp for that next commentary. Actually, he loved *driving* as two outings in the RAC Rally (1996 and 1999) proved. He crashed out of both but attacked each event with gusto.

As Brundle's racing career wound down, he seemed to become busier off-track. In addition to the broadcasting career, he took on management duties, forming 2MB with former

At Le Mans in 2012, Martin shared the Greaves Motorsport Zytek Z11SN-Nissan with his son, Alex, and Lucas Ordóñez. Their reward was 15th overall and ninth in the LMP2 class.

teammate Mark Blundell and they looked after the career of David Coulthard among others. With broadcasting and media work taking much of his time, Brundle resigned from 2MB and in 2009 moved to the BBC as ITV lost the rights to its coverage. Accolades came in broadcasting as well, as he was a Royal Television Society award winner four times. After a season paired with Jonathan Legard, Brundle was moved to be the lead commentator for

2011. The BBC, though, was under pressure to cut costs and when Sky Sports created its own dedicated F1 channel, Martin was headhunted to lead its presentation line-up. All of that came with a busy period as chairman of the BRDC which threw him into contract negotiations on behalf of Silverstone to retain its race. That meant he had to deal with Bernie Ecclestone on a business footing before interviewing him as a neutral broadcaster on a weekend.

His voice will be part of F1's television history but his efforts behind the wheel in Formula 1, sports cars and touring cars make him one of Britain's best, and perhaps underrated, drivers.

When F1 implemented famous names conducting post-qualifying and post-race interviews, Brundle's workload increased as, on occasions, he would have to dash from the box late-race to be in *parc ferme* to talk to the top three drivers. In 2016, as he raced from the Monaco commentary box to the podium, he suffered a mild heart attack and needed a 23 mm stent in his left anterior descending artery.

Undaunted, although he missed the next race in Canada, the then 57-year-old Brundle raced at Le Mans and took second in the Road to Le Mans support race. 'The cardio guy said, "You can do the race, just don't forget your blood thinners".'

His popular grid walks have become a trademark as he runs the gauntlet of security guards, celebrities without the first idea of who he is (or often what a Formula 1 race is) or drivers who want to be left alone, but it is compulsive viewing. Brundle says he dislikes doing them. After a chaotic visit to the Miami grid in 2022, where he mistook people and was shunned by others, he said: 'You have no idea how much I dislike doing them but somehow those crazy moments have defined my professional career.' His insight from the commentary box remains one of the highlights of the current era, especially as a new wave of drivers arrives to move the sport into a new age. He hasn't been afraid to offer opinions either. Take 2022 when news of Red Bull's budget overspend broke. Sky presenter Simon Lazenby offered the opinion that it had given Max Verstappen a second world championship and Brundle was vigorous in offering an alternative view: 'You can't say that, how can you say that? It wouldn't have done any harm so I hear what you're saying, but I don't think you can say slam dunk, that's two world championships won on £400,000.'

His voice will be part of F1's television history but his efforts behind the wheel in Formula 1, sports cars and touring cars make him one of Britain's best, and perhaps underrated, drivers.

For ITV, the BBC and Sky Sports, Martin Brundle has become a popular and authoritative voice on Formula 1 for viewers worldwide.

Three! Dario Franchitti poses for the cameras the morning after his third Indianapolis 500 win.

Full name	George Dario Marino Franchitti
Birthdate	19 May 1973
Place of birth	Bathgate

Dario Franchitti conquered America like no other
Brit before or since, mastering a discipline – oval
racing – that was a truly foreign concept.

If motor racing is about maximising opportunities, Dario Franchitti has done just that. From being one of many British Formula 1 hopefuls in the early 1990s, Franchitti maximised a chance offered to him in German Touring Car racing and turned it into a career in America that earned him success and fame.

George Dario Marino Franchitti can look back on a career that netted three Indianapolis 500 wins, four IndyCar drivers' titles and two wins in the Daytona 24 Hours sports car classic. From humble origins, Dario started racing as a 10-year-old in karts, encouraged by his father George who had raced in his youth before concentrating on running the family ice cream parlour. Franchitti's debut was not an auspicious one as his maiden race for the West of Scotland Kart Club resulted in an engine failure after just two laps, but young Dario was determined to become a racing driver, and aged 11, won the Scottish Junior Championship. A year later, the Franchitti name was attached to the British Junior Championship, a title he won in both 1985 and 1986. A year later, he was racing in the Karting World Championship before Scottish and British senior karting titles followed. In total, Franchitti's CV boasts 100 race wins and 20 karting championship successes.

The talent was spotted, and then nurtured, by David Leslie Senior who was running a race team and

Dario secured the British Formula Vauxhall crown in 1993 on his way through the junior single-seater ranks.

suggested that Dario come to the team and work on the cars and then put him behind the wheel of one. In 1991, Vauxhall backed a new junior single-seater initiative, Formula Vauxhall Junior, and Franchitti was on the grid for David Leslie Racing. The title was his after an end-of-season spurt that produced three wins in the last three races to make four victories in total, thus justifying the faith placed in him not only by Leslie but also Franchitti senior who had re-mortgaged the family house to help pay for Dario's season.

Again, the Scottish talent scouts came to Dario's aid. Paul Stewart Racing, overseen by triple Formula 1 World Champion Jackie Stewart,

offered Dario a test in a 2-litre Formula Vauxhall single-seater, the more powerful and aero-dependent cousin of the 1600cc Junior that Franchitti had mastered. Stewart offered to raise sponsorship from Scottish companies if Dario signed for the 1992 season and that faith was rewarded with fourth in the championship with podium finishes although a win went begging. Again, though, Franchitti's ability had opened eyes as he won the *Autosport* BRDC McLaren Young Driver of the Year Award at the end of the season and trousered £20,000 as part of his prize. He was handed his award by American racer Michael Andretti who was about to emulate his father Mario by entering Formula 1 for 1993 as teammate at McLaren to Ayrton Senna. While his year was disappointing, he and Dario would cross paths later . . . quite significantly.

By the end of 1993, Dario was Formula Vauxhall champion for PSR, four times a race winner and had wrapped up the title with three races to spare. The next rung on the ladder was Formula 3 where the PSR team looked after its Scottish charge, but Franchitti had a teammate with prodigious talent, Danish hot-shoe Jan Magnussen. Dario finished fourth, just one race win going his way, as Magnussen swept all before him to blast to the title. Suddenly, Franchitti's progress had been checked and it affected his ability to move up to Formula 3000 for 1995. Instead, Dario used a contact made during the *Autosport* BRDC McLaren Young Driver of the Year tests to discuss a career move with Mercedes: for 1995, he switched to touring cars and the DTM, the Deutsche Tourenwagen Meisterschaft. So popular was it with fans and promoters alike that more non-German tracks wanted a slice of the action, meaning that a second international mini-series was run. Dario drove for the D2-

AMG Mercedes team in one of the omnipotent C-Class saloons, equipped with anti-lock brakes and traction control. It was a big step up from an F3 car but Dario adapted well and took two pole positions in the DTM season along with a win in the ITC, the International Touring Car Championship, at the Italian track of Mugello. For 1996, the DTM had been consumed by the ITC and Dario won again in Suzuka on his way to fourth in the championship.

The writing was on the wall for the ITC, though. Manufacturers Mercedes, Opel and Alfa Romeo were spending money like it was going out of fashion and building outlandish cars that were costing fortunes to run. The bubble had to burst and when it did, there were plenty of drivers hunting drives for 1997 in Europe. Dario, though, had other ideas: he wanted to race in the USA. America's open-wheel series, then the CART World Series (CART being Championship Auto Racing Teams), was booming having had a spotlight turned on it in 1993 when reigning Formula 1 World Champion Nigel Mansell came to race in it. Dario maintained his Mercedes link by driving a Mercedes-powered Reynard 97i for Hogan Racing, the team owned by trucking magnate Carl Hogan who had received a letter of recommendation for young Dario from Jackie Stewart. It was a shrewd move and opened up a whole new chapter in Dario's life, not just on-track. He had tracks to learn and a new culture to adapt to and he also found himself on the same grid as Michael Andretti, no longer handing out awards but trying to fend off the Scottish upstart.

That maiden season was a tough one and Dario and Hogan didn't gel. After a number of incidents but with a pole and a fastest lap, plus Dario having already signed for Barry Green's Team Green for 1998, Hogan sacked Franchitti before the final race. The following season, Dario was back on the grid and in an environment that suited him as he bagged six top 10 finishes, three early-season poles and won at Road America to become the first Scottish winner

Three weeks later he won again, this time in Vancouver, and he also won the rain-shortened Houston race before the end of the season.

since his hero Jim Clark had won at Indianapolis in 1965. Three weeks later he won again, this time in Vancouver, and he also won the rain-shortened Houston race before the end of the season. Third was his reward in the championship and his reputation had soared, so much so that he was signing contract extensions as Barry Green fended off the pens of rival team managers.

One decision that Dario took was to remain in America rather than sign a deal to drive for Stewart's new Formula 1 team, Franchitti taking advice from Craig Pollock, his manager and the man behind Jacques Villeneuve's rise through the Champ Car ranks to Formula 1. It was a decision that worked out well as he won three races in 1999 and was in contention for the championship, taking the title fight to Juan Pablo Montoya in the final race, the pair ending the season tied on points but Montoya, with seven wins to Dario's three, bagged the crown.

That disappointment was compounded in early 2000 when he crashed heavily at the Homestead-Miami Speedway. In the impact, part of the car's suspension whacked him on the head and hence, in addition to fractures in his pelvis

Dario raced for Team Green in the 2001 FedEx Championship Series, taking his Reynard 01i-Honda to seventh in the championship.

and left hip, he suffered minor brain contusions. That meant his mental concentration, balance, memory and fatigue levels were all affected and he had to undergo physical therapy five times a week before the championship's doctor passed him fit to race. In a poor season blighted by accidents, team personnel switching, a lack of pre-season testing and an unreliable car, he was just 13th in the championship. A year later and back to full fitness, Dario took a win and seventh in the championship and in 2002 won in Vancouver and Montreal before a significant win came his way: he won on home soil in Rockingham's second and final Champ Car race, the UK's oval track having been built with the aim of enticing American racing to the British Isles. It was his first oval track victory, although more would come and of greater significance.

By now, American open-wheel racing was in civil war. On one side was CART and its established championship. On the other, Tony George, who ran Indianapolis had created his own series based on ovals with the Indianapolis 500 as its showcase race. It was called the Indy Racing League, IRL, and after an underwhelming start gradually grew, largely because the CART teams struggled to attract sponsorship to a series that didn't include Indy. George, as he had gambled, watched the teams gradually come to his grid. Franchitti made his debut in the IRL as a one-off at Indy in 2002 but a puncture condemned him to 19th place. A year later he was on the grid full-time, despite wanting to remain with CART for its greater variety of tracks. He signed for Andretti Green Racing, the Green being Barry's brother Kim and the Andretti being the same man who handed him an award in 1992. Now, Michael was team boss and Dario had to deliver for him.

Dario won the Daytona 24 Hours at his first attempt. His Riley MkX1-Lexus won by two laps.

IRL gave Dario a new challenge as it ran purely on the super-speedway ovals, fast and banked with an unforgiving wall inches away on the outside. Franchitti changed his driving style for the circuits and for the nature of the lighter V8-engined cars and finished seventh at the start of the season but then headed to Scotland for a break and hurt himself in a motorbike accident, an anterior stable compression fracture of the lumbar vertebrae being the medical name for a lot of pain. Although he returned to racing briefly, keyhole surgery ended his season early.

Results seemed harder to come by over the next seasons, but in 2007 Dario's confidence was unlocked after a win in a rain-shortened Indianapolis 500. To win America's biggest open-wheel race is a huge deal and Dario's face beamed out of news outlets the following morning. 'It was a feeling of relief,' he told British newspaper *Motorsport News*. 'I got the impression that it was never going to happen. It's the one thing I've done in my life that rather than the motivation tailing off, the motivation got stronger.' With that win under his belt, the rest of the IRL season went well for Dario and after wins at

Results seemed harder to come by over the next seasons, but in 2007 Dario's confidence was unlocked after a win in a rain-shortened Indianapolis 500.

Iowa and Richmond, he won his first American championship.

Suddenly, Dario's stock increased. He was in demand, on and off the track. There was an approach to race in the NASCAR series, America's Days of Thunder-style stock car series and the handful of races in which he drove rather upset Andretti Green Racing which didn't want to risk its star driver. He tried his hand at NASCAR in 2008, labelling his attempt at the Daytona 500 'a nightmare', but a year later Dario opted to return to IndyCar and its variety of circuits and away from the oval based IRL. It was a good move, as he won in Long Beach early in the season and blasted his way to the 2009 championship for Childress Ganassi Racing. A year later and the Franchitti legend gained another chapter: a second Indy 500 win was his and a second consecutive championship crown

'As he spun backwards the back of his car and the back of my car made contact so for a fraction of a second I got quite sideways.'

ended his season on a high. It was three titles in a row in 2011 when he defeated Australian Will Power to take the title once more. A rule change prompted a new car for 2012, as the Dallara DW12 broke cover. Dario struggled to adapt to the new car but he won the race that mattered, the Indy 500 once more. It was a close call as Takuma Sato attacked Dario for the lead on the last lap, lost it and crashed. 'As he spun backwards the back of his car and the back of my car made contact so for a fraction of a second I got quite sideways.'

The rest of the season was frustrating and 2013 was little better and ended in the worst possible way with Dario involved in a colossal accident in Houston. Sato was involved again and became sideways, Franchitti clipping the rear of his car and being launched into the catch-fencing. A section of fence was ripped apart, debris flew into the grandstands, Franchitti's

car was destroyed and 13 fans were injured from flying debris. Franchitti suffered concussion, two spinal fractures and a fractured right ankle. The concussion was bad: 'I lost five weeks of my life,' he said in an interview with Graham Bensinger. 'I remember my friend's wedding two weekends before and then . . . that's it.' Ultimately, he was advised that the injuries and those received from earlier crashes placed him at risk of permanent paralysis and brain damage if he had another accident. Reluctantly, Dario Franchitti hung up his helmet.

The legacy was of the British driver who took on America and conquered its toughest races. Not only were there those three Indianapolis wins, he also raced in the Daytona 24 Hours, America's sports car classic. After two previous attempts, in 2008 he won alongside Juan Pablo Montoya, Scott Pruett and Memo Rojas and Dario also raced in Australian Touring Cars as in 2010 the Surfers Paradise event welcomed an international co-driver for the regulars. By 2019, though, doctors had relented a little in the gloom of his condition and he returned to the circuits in historic events and in 2021 he made his Le Mans debut, not in the 24 Hours but in a support race. It was still a thrill for a huge enthusiast.

Dario's time in America achieved more than just winning races and titles. He married actress Ashley Judd whom he met at Jason Priestley's wedding in 1999. They were engaged that year and married in 2001, but they divorced in 2013. That prompted a return to the UK and a second marriage to hedge fund manager Eleanor Robb with whom he has two children. He became a popular voice in the animated movie *Turbo* and was a regular guest on the *Late Show with David Letterman* and *The Late Late Show with Craig Ferguson* as he made the move from the sports' pages to mainstream awareness. Once the helmet was hung up, he was recruited to join the commentary team for the new electric Formula E Series and was a presenter for

Four championship titles added to Dario Franchitti's three Indy 500 wins.

Dario Franchitti makes a pit stop on his way to winning the 2012 Indy 500 at Indianapolis Motor Speedway.

some of Goodwood's television output, plus fronting a series for Channel 4 in the UK with Take That band member Howard Donald, another car enthusiast and racer.

While all drivers are aware that danger stalks the sport, it has touched Franchitti more than many. Not just in terms of his own career-halting accident, but in 1999 his close friend Greg Moore was killed at the California Speedway. 'Greg was my best pal from the point that we first met, it was literally my first test at Homestead in 1997. We raced each other hard on the track and then had a laugh about it afterwards.'

More tragedy came in 2011 when another friend was killed, Dan Wheldon. It was in the final race of the 2011 season and Dario was fighting Will Power for the championship, but on lap 13 Wheldon was involved in a huge pile-up in which he lost his life. The race was abandoned and no result declared, meaning Dario was champion on the day that he lost another friend. That Dario raced on, that he *wanted* to carry on, perhaps illustrates that selfish competitive streak drivers need, but it is more reminiscent of a bygone and more dangerous age than present day racing.

Indeed, one could argue that Franchitti was born in the wrong era. For many drivers, the sport began the day they discovered it, but Dario was always fascinated by the history of it all. He would have loved to be a driver in the 1960s when they would race in many different categories on the same day, and one can picture Franchitti leaping from a single-seater to a sports car without batting an eyelid. He never saw Jim Clark race, but the Scotsman was Franchitti's hero and to emulate him by winning Indianapolis was a proud moment. Put Dario in a historic race paddock and he is in his element, wallowing in the nostalgia, fascinated by the cars of the time and relishing a chance to drive anything that he can. To drive Jim's Indy 500-winning Lotus 38 was a special moment, and his fascination for Clark culminated in him tracking down BJH 417B, the Lotus Cortina in which Clark won the 1964 British Saloon Car Championship. Dario listed it as one of his prized possessions, but presented it to the Jim Clark Room, the museum dedicated to Clark in Scotland. If he could appreciate Clark, so should other people.

In some ways, Franchitti had a charmed life. His movie star looks opened doors and his charm and business-savvy made him in demand from sponsors. He was able to translate that knowledge of the sport and easy-going nature to the commentary booth and his successes gained him an MBE in 2014 for 'Services to motor racing' as well as being made a vice-president of the British Racing Drivers' Club.

Franchitti didn't just achieve huge success in his chosen area of the sport but illustrated that there is more to motor racing than Formula 1 and a career, and a good one, can be made outside if opportunities are exploited. For some, Franchitti's will be a name that means nothing because he never appeared in a grand prix and, therefore, never came on to the radar, but in reality, Dario Franchitti is a driver who showed his ability in single-seaters and saloon cars, on ovals, road courses and street circuits, in endurance racing and historic events.

If Dario Franchitti is an unknown to some, he is unquestionably immortal to those who share his love, knowledge and enthusiasm for a sport that has given him the highest of highs and lowest of lows.

The most successful Formula 1 driver with over 100 wins to his name. Lewis Hamilton is as eager to win as ever.

LEWIS HAMILTON

Full name	Lewis Carl Davidson Hamilton
Birthdate	7 January 1985
Place of birth	Stevenage

Lewis Hamilton broke records and taboos as he
stormed to over 100 grand prix wins and became
a hero and celebrity in equal measure.

Lewis Hamilton attacked Formula 1 statistics like a fast bowler against an open wicket. Once he burst on to a grand prix grid, he looked like a champion and came oh-so close to being world beater in his debut season of 2007. By the end of 2023 he had the most wins, 103, the most pole positions (103) and the most podium finishes, 191. And, crucially, he shows no sign of letting up.

Lewis Carl Davidson Hamilton was a proficient footballer and cricketer at school but it was on four wheels that he made his mark, leaving an impression not only on the sport but on the world itself. More than a racing driver, Hamilton contributed to raising awareness of racism and human rights, as well as being a fashion icon. While some of his detractors prefer him to race cars and steer away from his personality lifestyle, Hamilton's view on life has made him big news in the mainstream media as much as the sports press and say 'Lewis' now and people know exactly who you mean. The Hamilton can be left unsaid.

Aged eight, Lewis was bought his first kart with which to go racing, and he mopped up the British Cadet Karting title in 1995 before he blitzed his way through the karting categories. With an impressive reputation behind him, he jumped into car racing but skipped the first rung on the ladder, Formula Ford, to go straight into the greater downforce Formula Renault category and finished

Where it all began. Buckmore Park, 1995. Lewis Hamilton leads karting rival Mike Conway.

third in the British series. Formula 3 beckoned a year later but Lewis, guided by father Anthony who had earlier taken on four different jobs simultaneously to pay for his son's racing, elected to stay in Formula Renault. Ten wins, 11 pole positions and nine fastest laps proved it was the right move. He made his Formula 3 debut at the end of the season at Brands Hatch but a puncture in race one was followed by a collision with teammate Tor Graves in race two that necessitated a trip to hospital. After racing in the prestigious Macau F3 Grand Prix that autumn, he was placed in the German-based F3 Euro Series for 2004, by now under the watchful eye of Mercedes and, principally, McLaren supremo Ron Dennis. Hamilton had introduced himself to Dennis at a motor racing awards ceremony as a 10-year-old and said: 'Hi, I'm Lewis Hamilton, and I've just won the British Karting Championship, and one day I want to be Formula 1 World Champion in your car.' Dennis was impressed in his confidence and kept an eye on him, helping him to the title in 2005 in which he took 15 wins as well as adding coveted F3 one-off wins such as the Pau Grand Prix and the Marlboro Masters at Zandvoort. A year later, he was in GP2, the last rung below F1 and again he destroyed the opposition: with five wins he was champion, including an outstanding win at Silverstone which underlined his bravery as he darted through traffic to grab the lead. By the end of the season he was on the cusp of Formula 1.

Dennis decided the time was right: Hamilton became a Formula 1 driver for 2007 in the McLaren MP4-22 Mercedes and he underlined his potential by qualifying fourth and finishing third for his first race in Australia. It took until just round six in Canada before he took his first pole and a day later he secured his first win. As Formula 1's first black driver he was always under the spotlight, but finally it wasn't due to the racism he had suffered at school but as a grand prix star. By the end of the season,

Hamilton clinched the 2003 Formula Renault UK title as his reputation grew.

he was in the fight for the world championship but a gearbox problem dropped him to 18th place and he missed out by just one point to Kimi Räikkönen. A year later he put that right, a last-gasp move on Timo Glock on the final lap of the Brazilian Grand Prix giving him the title by one point and denying race winner Felipe Massa the crown, making him the youngest world champion at the time at 23 years and 300 days. That season, Hamilton won the British Grand Prix on a soaking wet Silverstone circuit. Sitting in a ball of spray generated by the leading McLaren of teammate Heikki Kovalainen, it took him just four-and-a-half laps to move ahead. Within a lap he was 2.4 seconds clear of the pack, by the end of the 60-lap race he was over 68 seconds clear and just two other cars finished on the lead lap. It was the biggest winning margin for over a decade. It also marked the first

> It was the biggest winning margin for over a decade. It also marked the first of a record eight British Grand Prix wins.

of a record eight British Grand Prix wins. Again, Hamilton and numbers . . . records were created, broken and broken again as he swept through the sport.

The wide-eyed innocent kid who arrived at McLaren in 2007 was soon replaced by a canny operator. As teammate to Fernando Alonso, then a double world champion, Lewis was in no mood to play second-fiddle and regarded McLaren as his team: after all, his career had been masterminded by the Woking squad. In Hungary in 2007, harmony fell apart. Hamilton had prevented Alonso from passing him in the qualifying session when it was Alonso's turn to get a longer fuel burn. As the cars pitted, Alonso hesitated when released and that delayed Hamilton to the point where he missed one final lap as the chequered flag greeted him. Eventually, the stewards agreed that Alonso had impeded Hamilton and docked the Spaniard five grid places, allowing Lewis to start from pole, but more importantly a marker had been laid down. Don't mess . . .

As Hamilton established himself at McLaren, the wins continued but he felt that he was just an employee after comments by Ron Dennis.

McLaren nurtured the young Hamilton and it was for Ron Dennis' team that he scored his first grand prix win in Canada, 2007.

He was also being courted by rival teams. Having bought the Brawn team, Mercedes was now on the grid as a constructor, not just an engine supplier, and the Brackley-based team had its eyes on Hamilton and he signed for 2013. It was the start of a stunning partnership, winning the world championship in 2014, 2015, 2017, 2018, 2019 and 2020. That seventh world championship matched another record – Michael Schumacher's seven world titles – but it is a record he wants to break.

His relationship with Mercedes teammate Nico Rosberg was another fascinating one. Rosberg was the incumbent Mercedes driver when Hamilton arrived in 2013. They had been teammates in karting, raced against each other in F3 and now lined up as teammates in F1. Hamilton won the championship in 2014, the first year of turbo-hybrid engines, and Rosberg knew he would have to dig deep to better his biggest rival. Take Barcelona 2016 when the pair tangled on the opening lap of the grand prix but in Abu Dhabi that year Hamilton was guilty of backing Rosberg into traffic in the hope that the pack behind would then overtake Nico and in turn help Hamilton win the title. While some found that sneaky, it was a racer racing, it was Hamilton's mind in overdrive. He was leading and could do no better, points-wise. What he needed was for Rosberg to score fewer points and for that to happen, he needed him to drop back.

Hamilton in a race car is a fascinating beast, especially in adversity. Take Silverstone 2021. Lewis was determined to win on home soil and determined that Max Verstappen, his new arch-rival, would not be leaving Silverstone with the winner's trophy. Things came to a head on the opening lap

Hamilton loves his fans and they love him. When he wins the British Grand Prix, he knows how to celebrate. This was the reaction in 2019.

when they touched at Copse and Max was spat off the road. Hamilton was given a 10-second penalty for his part in the accident and yet from a distant fifth, initially complaining about the car, he charged back into contention to grab the lead two laps from home. Or Spain that year: 'It's insane, man. They've got so much more grip,' he told his team of the Red Bulls. By flagfall, he was the winner by over 15 seconds. Monaco 2019 on tyres: 'I'm driving super slow and I'm not sure they are going to last.' He won. Back Hamilton into a corner and his default setting seems to be to fear the worst, but then that brings out the best in him. That Silverstone charge from 2021 is a perfect example as his initial radio traffic hinted at him believing retirement, not a win, was the expected outcome.

Errors aren't common in Hamilton's career. In 2011, though, there were some clumsy moments as he faced a tough opponent in Sebastian Vettel, the Red Bull driver heading to the world championship title. Three times that year he was handed a penalty for being involved in an incident and three times he collided with Felipe Massa's Ferrari. The least said about colliding with teammate Jenson Button in Canada,

Back Hamilton into a corner and his default setting seems to be to fear the worst, but then that brings out the best in him.

the better. That season, also affected by dramas in his personal life and his on-off relationship with pop singer Nicole Scherzinger, included an outstanding win in Abu Dhabi, proving that he hadn't lost his touch.

And that continued through his Mercedes time, Rosberg's season aside. Bear in mind that the sheer commitment and will needed to defeat Hamilton over just one season prompted Rosberg to retire with the world championship in his pocket. The thought of going through all that again and again was enough to make Rosberg reconsider life.

One cannot discuss Hamilton the driver without looking at Hamilton the man and in that, inevitably, comes the topic of race. He suffered racial abuse at school and was told by his father that the best way to respond was on-track. Lewis didn't have many people to talk to anyway: raised by his white mother Carmen Larbalestier

By 2020, though, not only was the world different but so was Hamilton. He was an established star, a multiple world champion, a face known by millions.

until he was 12, he then went to live with his father. 'I did karate because I was being beaten up and I wanted to defend myself,' he said. That racism followed him into Formula 1, especially when Spanish Fernando Alonso-supporting fans took against him and painted themselves black and wore wigs, but he tried to turn the topic upside down when repeated visits to the race stewards were met with his response: 'Maybe it's because I'm black, that's what Ali G says!' He was joking but it came across falteringly.

By 2020, though, not only was the world different but so was Hamilton. He was an established star, a multiple world champion, a face known by millions. His social media following was off the scale. When he spoke, people listened. That May, 46-year-old American George Floyd was murdered by a policeman after being arrested. It sparked protests and riots in America, all at a time when coronavirus-induced

lockdowns were gripping most countries. By July, sport was starting up, and Hamilton used his profile to raise awareness of the burgeoning Black Lives Matter movement which was gathering momentum around the world. Hamilton took the knee on the grid of every grand prix that season but was quick to point out that, initially, he was the only person doing so. He galvanised Formula 1 management who introduced an End Racism campaign, with drivers joining together for a pre-race photo wearing t-shirts bearing the End Racism legend. That this happened at all was down to Hamilton's stance through Black Lives Matter. Later that season, he appeared on the podium at Mugello with a t-shirt that said: 'Arrest the cops who killed Breonna Taylor'. The 26-year-old African American woman had been fatally shot when at least seven police officers forced their way into her apartment as part of a drug dealing investigation. This time the FIA, the sport's governing body, clamped down on Hamilton's attire, but his crusade was highlighting not just the issue of racism but Hamilton's desire to end it. He deserves credit, too, for convincing Mercedes at board level to paint the so-called

Silver Arrows black for two seasons to highlight the campaign.

He was outspoken in criticising racing in Bahrain with its poor human rights record and likewise he went public with reservations about racing in Hungary and Saudi Arabia, countries with a poor history for gay and lesbian rights. Others may have supported his views privately, but it was Hamilton who had the courage to speak out first.

In 2020 as well, he launched The Hamilton Commission with the Royal Academy of Engineering with the aim of finding more ways in motorsport to encourage people from black backgrounds. In 2021,

A familiar sight as Hamilton wins again for Mercedes. This is Barcelona in 2019.

he became the first recipient of the new Laureus Athlete Advocate of the Year Award for his involvement in fighting racism and he launched Mission 44, a charitable foundation created to help youngsters from underprivileged backgrounds achieve their ambitions. He pledged £20 million of his own wealth to the programme.

But for a man who isn't afraid of airing opinions, it was his ability to maintain a dignified silence that is one of his defining factors. In December 2021, the Formula 1 World Championship came down to the wire in Abu Dhabi. It was Hamilton against the pretender to his throne, the

With his childhood karting rival Nico Rosberg (left) and Daniel Ricciardo in 2014.

exciting and prodigiously talented Max Verstappen. Hamilton was leading, Verstappen was behind when Nicolas Latifi crashed his Williams triggering a late-race safety car period. Verstappen, with nothing to lose, was called into the pits for new tyres. Hamilton had everything to lose: if he had pitted, Verstappen would have stayed out and jumped ahead, and once the Dutchman had served his stop there was no way Mercedes could pit a lap later because Lewis would have fallen behind Verstappen. It was touch and go whether there was time for the race to restart, but the FIA Race Director Michael Masi seemed keen to reignite the battle. A regulation stated that lapped cars may be allowed to overtake the safety car and regain their lost lap, but then an extra lap is needed before the safety car is withdrawn. Masi allowed only certain cars to unlap themselves and then called in the safety car on that lap. It meant a one-lap dash to the flag with Verstappen on brand new tyres, Hamilton on old ones. There was no contest as Verstappen flashed past and scored to a maiden F1 title. 'This has been manipulated, man,' said Hamilton to the

Hamilton heads into battle, his time at Mercedes being a hugely successful period with six world titles won. His initial title came with McLaren.

team over the radio, and while Hamilton's team boss Toto Wolff was incandescent, Lewis was the model of control and magnanimity. After sitting motionless in his car for over two minutes, he had to face the world and offered: 'A big congratulations to Max and to his team.' To his credit, he went to the podium and stood on the second step, not for Hamilton the trick of standing on the winner's position to underline a point. A more dignified defeat sport has barely seen and while he lost the championship that day, he won many admirers for his conduct.

But for a man who isn't afraid of airing opinions, it was his ability to maintain a dignified silence that is one of his defining factors.

Knighted in 2021, Hamilton is constantly evolving, maturing. He is a more confident person, more careful in what he says. Gone are gaffes such as taking a selfie while riding a Harley Davidson or referring to his hometown of Stevenage as 'The Slums'. Now he is savvy enough to accept that

This, coming after the huge disappointment of Abu Dhabi 2021, could have led Hamilton to spit dummies or walk from the sport.

travelling the world while focused on climate change doesn't sit well, so the private jet has gone and his fashion line with Tommy Hilfiger has to be sustainable. The image is different now too. Compare photos of the 2007 rookie, clean-cut and innocent, with the current Hamilton with his multitudinous tattoos and piercings coupled to his rapper image. He has revealed music is a passion and

has invested as a movie producer in a Formula 1-themed film set to star Brad Pitt, this coming on the back of a nascent music career which includes playing on Christina Aguilera's 2018 track 'Pipe' under the pseudonym XNDA, although it was two years after its release before he admitted it was him. 'I shied away from acknowledging it was me, I don't know why, maybe insecurities, fear, overthinking, something I think many people can relate to . . .'

In 2022, Hamilton faced something alien to him: a winless season in Formula 1. Worse, the Mercedes-AMG team had a tough season with a difficult car and it was his teammate, rising star George Russell, who scored honours in Brazil. This, coming after the huge disappointment of Abu Dhabi 2021, could have led Hamilton to spit dummies or walk from the sport, but despite branding the Mercedes W13 car as 'undriveable', his work ethic shone through and gradually the car became closer to the pace of Red Bull.

As the sport moves on, Hamilton faces another tough challenger: Max Verstappen. Twice he has lost a world championship to the Dutchman but remember

On his way to a record-equalling seventh title in 2020.

In 2021 Hamilton very nearly captured an eighth World Championship, scoring eight GP victories, but he would be denied in controversial circumstances.

that Lewis saw off Fernando Alonso from McLaren, defeated Jenson Button in the same stable and put Sebastian Vettel in his place when the German left Red Bull for Ferrari. World champions all, of course. Whether it be in a race or a championship fight or car development, a defensive Hamilton comes out stronger and after two defeats and a winless season, the hunger in him seems as strong as ever, maybe more so as he aims to show the world that he isn't finished yet. He has, inevitably, grown up since his Formula 1 debut back in 2007 and the confidence is as much in the car as out of it. He is F1's only true megastar with a global reach of over one billion on Instagram and has a fan base that includes people who have no interest in the sport, but in him as a human being. The desire to win, to break more records and to be the benchmark in his chosen sport is as strong as ever, but so too is a desire to improve the world. A trailblazer, he has redefined what a racing driver is, how they behave and also the level at which they best operate. The GOAT, Greatest Of All Time? It's hard to argue.

HONOURABLE MENTIONS

For a country that has spawned so many stars of motor racing, whittling a list of drivers to 12 was hardly the work of a moment. Even harder, perhaps, was the list of honourable mentions which is the equivalent to volume two of this book. Each has enjoyed meritorious careers in his own right.

Richard Seaman, born 4 February 1913, was arguably Britain's first grand prix hero in a career that pre-dated the Formula 1 World Championship. Seaman was still maturing as a driver when he was killed in the Belgian Grand Prix aboard a Mercedes-Benz and became the centre of all manner of posthumous prognostications thanks to the mood of the time: it was 1939 when he was killed and the largest wreath at his funeral came from Adolf Hitler. He had triumphed the previous year in the German Grand Prix and, as a consequence, had been obliged to proffer a Nazi salute in victory on the podium. He had little option, but the moment was immortalised

Richard Seaman

with the dashing Englishman seemingly on the wrong side of history. His rise to grand prix racing, no such thing as Formula 1 back then, was as swift as it could be for a wealthy amateur. Inspired by racer and record holder Henry Segrave, Dick was happier reading PG Wodehouse's Jeeves and Wooster novels than academic materials, but he was far from unintelligent. In September 1931 Richard Seaman was on the line at Shelsley Walsh, the popular British hillclimb venue, aboard his Riley and was second – of two – in the 1100cc sports car class. It was not an auspicious debut, but he persevered and with a Delage and an ERA took wins in the British Empire Trophy and the British Grand Prix at Donington. For 1937, against the wishes of his long-suffering mother, to whom Seaman would go when in need of more money for his racing, he signed for Alfred Neubauer's Mercedes team and won the 1938 German Grand Prix as well as taking second in Switzerland and third in Britain.

It was in the wet Belgian weather a year later that he crashed into a tree and unconscious and with a broken arm was unable to extricate himself from his burning car. In excruciating pain he was taken to hospital and was able to converse with visitors that night but the effects of the burns began to take hold and his major organs started to shut down. He died that night, eight hours after the crash. He was

26. Remembered by an annual race with the Vintage Sports-Car Club, his was a career terminated long before his true ability could shine.

Mike Hawthorn, the bow tie and flat 'at-wearing racing driver known as 'The Farnham Flyer', was Britain's first Formula 1 World Champion and yet often ignored for his achievements. Born on 10 April 1929, he won but three grands prix, all for Ferrari, and won the Le Mans 24 Hours as well as many lesser events. Extrovert, beer-drinking and with a love of life, his persona was conflicted as

Mike Hawthorn

he suffered from a chronic kidney ailment and could be offensive to whoever he wished when the mood took him. Despite his on-track successes, the British media took against him for avoiding National Service, living in Italy (a former enemy nation) and enjoying life on the continent when his peers were serving Queen and country. They ignored the timeline and that Hawthorn's kidney condition left him unfit for National Service, but the accusations hurt. So did the suggestion it was his bad driving that triggered the worst accident in the sport's history at the 1955 Le Mans 24 Hours when he dived to the pits and the following Lance Macklin slowed so suddenly that Pierre Levegh's Mercedes used his Austin Healey 100S as a ramp and ploughed into the crowd killing 80 people. Hawthorn and Ivor Bueb won the race, but Hawthorn was vilified by the French press. His 1958 Formula 1 World Championship title came thanks to the generosity of Stirling Moss pointing out the mistake of the organisers and it is this that is remembered rather than Hawthorn's own ability. His world title won he retired on the spot and in January 1959 crashed to his death on the A31 driving towards Guildford. Having overtaken team entrant Rob Walker, Hawthorn was caught out on a damp patch of tarmac and, clipping an oncoming lorry, crashed into a tree. Hawthorn was dead within seconds.

Richard Attwood's Formula 1 results netted just one podium finish at Monaco in 1968 for BRM, but his sports car racing results make him one of Britain's top drivers. Born on 4 April 1940, Attwood started racing in 1960 aboard a Triumph TR3 but it was a win in the Monaco Grand

Richard Attwood

Attwood won Le Mans for Porsche in 1970.

Prix supporting Formula Junior race that shot him to fame. While single-seater drives came, it was in sports car racing that he scored results: a win in the 1965 Rand 9 Hours with David Piper in a Ferrari 365 P2 was just the start. He won the Rand 9 Hours again in 1966 and by 1969 was racing a works Porsche for the first time, the 908 model with Vic Elford and was second in the BOAC 500 at Brands Hatch.

By 1970, he found himself one of the drivers charged with taming the difficult Porsche 917. Now running in its short-tail guise, the car was shared with Hans Hermann and in wet conditions they took the Porsche Salzburg entry to honours. A year later he finished second at Le Mans in a Gulf-backed 917 but called time on his career at the end of the season. Except that Richard (he always hated the 'Dickie' moniker that over-familiar journalists gave him) never really retired. In 1984, he raced in top-line sports car racing for the Aston Martin Nimrod team, in the late 1980s he was to be found in the Porsche Club Great Britain's championship in a Porsche 944 Turbo and even aged 77, in 2017 he raced a Porsche 928 in British historic races as part of the car's 40th anniversary celebrations. In his eighties, Attwood worked as an instructor at the Porsche Centre at Silverstone and continued to race at Goodwood with undimmed enthusiasm.

🏴󠁧󠁢󠁳󠁣󠁴󠁿 Watson

John Watson

John Watson MBE won just five Formula 1 races but as he says: 'I survived 152 grands prix.' 'Wattie', born on 4 May 1946, raced in a dangerous era and suffered some big accidents along the way but took fine wins such as Long Beach in 1982 when he came from 22nd on the grid and his British Grand Prix win in 1981 which remains his proudest achievement. After F1 spat him out, Wattie turned his attention to sports car racing and broadcasting and for over three decades he has brought his keen eye and sometimes critical opinions to F1, touring cars and GT racing. His last grand prix came in 1985 but he remains in demand for his views on the sport because John has always been clever enough to say something to which people will listen, a soundbite. You won't always agree with him but you *will* listen. Never married, Wattie is a contradiction at times: fiercely competitive and a lover of an argument, yet one of his great passions is fishing where he can be in silence and solitude for hours on end. In the commentary box, he cares hugely about the broadcast and doing it well and yet hours of homework isn't for him. When my wife was hospitalised, Wattie's second question (after her health) was to enquire how my daughter, then seven, was coping. No-one else we knew asked that question and yet this was from a man generations her senior and without children.

Few have remained as passionate about F1 so many years after their retirement and it is that love of the sport, coupled with his natural affinity with a microphone, that has kept the charming Watson current so many years after his final race even if his successes are sometimes overlooked.

Steve Soper was a rare thing: someone who came from British club racing to become an internationally regarded, well-paid manufacturer driver in a golden age of touring car racing.

Soper, born on 27 September 1951, began racing Minis in one-make events and a modified Fiat X1/9 in modified sports cars before graduating to the British Saloon Car Championship in 1982 in an Austin Metro. For 1983, Soper drove a Rover Vitesse and scored more points than anyone else, but his title was lost amid arguments over car illegality the following summer. Soper didn't look back and was soon busy in the European championship for Rover, before switching to Rudi Eggenberger's crack team for 1986. He drove the Ford Sierra XR4Ti before the Cosworth and then the RS500 models hit the tracks the following season. Race wins came even if titles didn't, Steve being in demand by BMW after the Sierra's time came to an end. Soper drove for BMW in the German Touring Car Championship, the British, the Italian, the Asia Pacific, the Japanese (which he won in 1995) and was a BMW driver when he won the Spa 24 Hour and

twice the touring car race at the daunting Macau street circuit.

His BMW connection placed him in the McLaren F1-GTR in GT racing in the late 1990s with its BMW engine and in the BMW V12 LM. In 2001, having fallen out with BMW's motorsport head Gerhard Berger, Soper was back on the BTCC grid in an unsuccessful Peugeot 406 in a thin field. Results were hard to come by and a heavy accident led to his retirement on medical grounds. Over time, though, his diagnosis was good enough to allow him, now a BMW dealer, to return successfully to historic racing in all manner of touring cars and remind people why he was regarded as Britain's best-ever tin-top tussler.

Steve Soper

John Cleland

When **John Cleland,** born 15 July 1952, and Steve Soper tangled in the final round of the 1992 British Touring Car Championship it cost the loquacious Scotsman the title but made him a star. His angry description of Soper, 'The man's an animal' has lived with him ever since and their accident launched the BTCC to a new audience. Cleland, a car dealer, had come up from UK club racing to the BTCC in the days when it ran for four classes of car divided by engine size. He won it in 1989 and, as television coverage increased, became worth his PR weight in gold to employer Vauxhall.

Cleland had a smart mouth but could back up his talk with results. He was loyal to Vauxhall, even though he never sold their

cars, to win the BTCC in 1995 and continued to the end of the 1990s before frustration with an uncompetitive car prompted his retirement. He turned to his car dealership and to a microphone at World Touring Car Championship races before returning to racing in one of his old 1990s Vauxhall Vectras in historic touring car races, the car just as it was in period and Cleland and his sons, who prepared the car, all in period clothing. Cleland also found fame in Australia and second in the Bathurst 1000 race from 22nd on the grid was an outstanding effort. Cleland was already established in the BTCC as it grew: he was joined by former F1 drivers, sports car stars, up-and-coming talents and touring car champions and yet he was able to beat them all. It was tempting to forget just how good he was because he was that jolly Scottish bloke, but Cleland was an outstanding touring car racer who was absolutely vital to the success of the BTCC on television.

Derek Warwick fought off personal tragedy, politics and bad luck to become a world champion in Superstox (a British stock car category) and sports cars, to win Le Mans and to serve as a popular president of the British Racing Drivers' Club. He achieved success everywhere – except F1.

Never one to moan, Warwick, born 27 August 1954, came from the hard-knock school of Superstox into circuit racing and starred in Formula Ford and then Formula 3. He won races for Toleman in Formula 2 and moved up to F1 with the team in 1981 with the overweight Toleman TG181. Results were hard to come by but he shone in the 1982 British Grand Prix before the car let him down. He moved to Renault for 1984, a team in a slow decline as it transpired, but plans to join Lotus for 1986 were blocked by lead driver Ayrton Senna who didn't want a teammate who might rival

him. Instead, Warwick turned to sports cars and a Silk Cut Jaguar ride followed by an in-and-out spell of F1 as he subbed for drivers and found a permanent seat some seasons, as well as winning the Le Mans 24 Hours in 1992 for Peugeot. He raced in the British Touring Car Championship in an Alfa Romeo 155TS in 1995 but the car wasn't competitive and he formed his own team, Triple Eight Engineering, which became a powerhouse operating Vauxhalls successfully for many seasons.

Derek Warwick

In 1991, Derek's younger brother Paul was killed in a Formula 3000 accident at Oulton Park and while his death affected Derek greatly, he never lost his love of the sport as he continued to race and then act as a driver steward at grands prix and as president of the BRDC with a keen interest in helping young drivers.

Damon Hill

After the death of his father, **Damon Hill,** born 17 September 1960, couldn't benefit from any family help to go racing, but the former motorcycle courier did it the hard way. Just as his father had.

It was on bikes that he began racing but Brands Hatch supremo John Webb recognised, as he always did, when someone had promotional qualities and tempted him into car racing. Thus, a full season on four wheels came in Formula Ford in 1985 and he swiftly moved up to Formula 3 and Formula 3000. A test-driver role with Williams helped enhance his reputation that could have been mauled by a part season in a recalcitrant Brabham in 1992. As he was lapped by the dominant Nigel Mansell en route to victory, Damon was all but unnoticed but that changed the year after as he was in a Williams and won three races on the bounce. In 1994, he was forced, just like his father, to carry the team after the death of a teammate, Ayrton Senna being killed at Imola, and he went to the final race fighting Michael Schumacher for the crown. A clash between them ended Hill's hopes but he came back stronger to win the world championship in 1996

Hill carried his father's famous helmet colours to his own world title.

but was eased out by Frank Williams just as 1992 champ Nigel Mansell had been. Hill went to Arrows and then Jordan, winning for Eddie's eponymous team, but called time on his career at the end of 1999. After that, he served as president of the British Racing Drivers' Club, helping hugely in contract negotiations over its grand prix, as well as looking after his business interests. A return to Formula 1 came with a microphone as he joined Sky's extensive coverage of the sport as well as forming his own band, The Conrods. Hill admitted to suffering from depression after his retirement from driving

but will be best remembered for being the first second-generation Formula 1 World Champion.

Twice a Le Mans 24 Hours winner, **Allan McNish,** born 29 December 1969, could and should have achieved much in Formula 1 but fate wasn't on his side. An impressive junior career in Formula Ford 1600 catapulted him up the ranks to a Marlboro-backed spell in Formula Vauxhall and Formula Opel, then Formula 3 and Formula 3000 but it was here that his career stalled. Results were hard to come by and after being taken on by McLaren as a test driver, he was released meaning that he turned to Renault for equivalent employment. The hope was that he would get the call to the race team but that never came and an offer to race a Porsche in North America changed his life. He won the 1998 Le Mans 24 Hours for Porsche and switched to Audi in 2000. With the German constructor he had many chances, some left begging to win again at la Sarthe, but he did claim honours in 2008 and 2013 as well as racing for Audi in the DTM, the German-based touring car series. His sole F1 season was for Toyota in 2002 and there was much support to see the popular Scot on a grand prix grid at last. Toyota, though, underestimated the challenge ahead and produced a mediocre car and McNish was dropped at the end of the season.

It was in sports cars and with Audi that he made his name, taking the 2013 World Endurance Championship for the German constructor and being the team principal for Audi's Formula E project. He acted as a commentator on Formula 1 and sports car racing with an incisive racer's eye and served as a steward at a number of grands prix while adding driver management to his workload, but it was as a blindingly fast sports car racer that his reputation was cemented.

Jenson Button, born 19 January 1980, burst into Formula 1 on the crest of a wave when, in 2000, he signed for Williams. After an impressive karting career, he claimed the British Formula Ford title in 1998, won that year's Formula Ford Festival and then moved to Formula 3 in which he finished third in the championship. Aged just 20, he was a Formula 1 driver with high expectations and took eighth in the championship. Despite having a five-year contract, he was loaned to Benetton for 2002 before being

Allan McNish

Jenson Button

dropped and picked up by the BAR team which morphed into Honda for 2006. In Hungary that year he took his first win after 118 efforts and his confidence was boosted but the Japanese car maker's 2008 car was awful and Honda pulled out at the end of the year. Ross Brawn, though, had been working on the new-for-2009 regulations and was confident he had a car that could win and thus he bought the remnants of the team and retained Button who won six of the first seven races to gain an advantage. Eventually others caught up, but Button had done enough to win the title before jumping to McLaren. Wins followed before he retired from F1 at the end of 2017 and has since raced in rallycross, sports cars, GTs and historics. Awarded an MBE in 2010, he established the Jenson Button Trust which selects a number of charitable foundations to receive funding and is also part of Sky's Formula 1 coverage where his easy-going persona and ready wit has won him many fans. Button seldom seems to feature in the same breath as greats such as Ayrton Senna and Michael Schumacher but as a world champion he is undoubtedly one of British motor racing's true stars and hasn't finished with the sport yet.

BIBLIOGRAPHY

With a number of the drivers featured in these pages no longer with us, it has been necessary to draw on a number of different titles to help with their stories. The listing below represents sources for facts, clarifications, context, quotes and statistics.

Books

Bell, Derek and Henry, Alan, *My Racing Life*, Haynes Publishing, 2011.

Dodgins, Tony, *Autocourse 2014/15*, Icon Publishing, 2014.

Dodgins, Tony, *Autocourse 2016/17*, Icon Publishing, 2016.

Dodgins, Tony, *Autocourse 2020/21*, Icon Publishing, 2020.

Dodgins, Tony, *Autocourse 2021/22*, Icon Publishing, 2021.

Dodgins, Tony, *Autocourse 2022/23*, Icon Publishing, 2022.

Donaldson, Gerald, *Grand Prix People*, Motor Racing Publications, 1990.

Hamilton, Maurice, *Autocourse 1980/81*, Hazleton Publishing, 1980.

Hamilton, Maurice, *Autocourse 1986/87*, Hazleton Publishing, 1986.

Hamilton, Maurice, *Grand Prix British Winners*, Guinness Publishing, 1991.

Hayhoe, David, *Formula 1 The Knowledge*, David Hayhoe Publications, 2016.

Hayhoe, David and Holland, David, *Grand Prix Data Book 4th Edition*, Haynes Publishing, 2006.

Henry, Alan, *Autocourse 1988/89*, Hazleton Publishing, 1988.

Henry, Alan, *Autocourse 1992/93*, Hazleton Publishing, 1992.

Henry, Alan, *Autocourse 1995/96*, Hazleton Publishing, 1995.

Henry, Alan, *Autocourse 1996/97*, Hazleton Publishing, 1996.

Henry, Alan, *Autocourse 2007/08*, CMG Publishing, 2007.

Henry, Alan, *Autocourse 2008/09*, CMG Publishing, 2008.

Henry, Alan, *Driving Forces*, PSL, 1992.

Hodges, David, *A-Z of Formula Racing Cars*, Bay View Books, 1990.

Jones, Bruce, *The Formula One Record Book 2023 Edition*, Welbeck Publishing, 2023.

Khan, Mark, *Death Race Le Mans 55*, Barrie & Jenkins Ltd, 1976.

Marshall, Gerry and Walton, Jeremy, *Only Here for the Beer*, Haynes Publishing, 1978.

Moss, Stirling and Hailwood, Mike, *Racing and all That*, Pelham Books, 1980.

Nye, Doug, *Racers 1948 – 1968 The Legends of Formula 1*, Queensgate Publications, 1999.

Rubython, Tom, *Shunt – The Story of James Hunt*, The Myrtle Press, 2010.

Scherer, Peter, *50 Years of British Grand Prix Drivers*, TFM Publishing, 1999.

Small, Steve, *Grand Prix Who's Who*, Icon Publishing, 2012.

Stanley, Louis, *Behind the Scenes*, Queen Anne Press, 1985.

Stanley, Louis, *Strictly off the Record*, Salamander Books, 1999.

Walton, Jeremy, *Gerry Marshall: His Authorised Biography*, Haynes Publishing, 2010.

Williams, Richard, *A Race with Love and Death*, Simon & Schuster, 2020.

Magazines

Autosport
BRDC Bulletin
Motorsport News
Motor Sport
Private Eye

Newspapers

Daily Express
Daily Telegraph
Evening Standard
The Express
The Sun

Websites

Autosport.com
Btcc.net
Formula1.com

Two of the greats together. Jackie Stewart and John Surtees share a joke.

ACKNOWLEDGEMENTS

When I am asked how one should get started in motor racing commentary, I find myself having to admit that an element of it is luck. Right place, right time. So it was in the gestation of this book as I found myself at a race in Australia in 2000 and made a friendship which took me back there over a number of years. When one of those old friends, fellow commentator Luke West, came calling with an idea for a book in 2022, it was thanks to a relationship built in a commentary box on the other side of the world a decade earlier.

To Luke for his recommendation, I am hugely grateful just as I am for his suggestions, support and guidance. To the team at Rockpool Publishing/Gelding Street Press, my thanks are due as they have patiently borne with a rookie author and smiled patiently as deadlines were missed like a corner apex by a novice driver. Sorry! Editor Brooke Halliwell has also worked her magic by taking my motor-racing-based word salad and turned it into something readable.

In selecting my Immortals, my old friend *Motorsport News* editor Matt James has been a tremendous sounding board. He has argued with me, cast an eye over my words and then argued again and to him I am grateful, especially as this process went in tandem with his own book project.

It would be churlish not to thank those who nurtured the interest of a small boy all those years ago. Margaret Simpson and her late husband, David, provided tickets to an Oulton Park race meeting in 1977 and the damage was done. For years afterwards, my parents, Roy and Valerie, acted as a taxi service to Oulton and elsewhere, as did family friend Robin Booth before he returned to racing himself in Formula Ford.

And, in the selfish world that is motorsport, my wife Dawn and daughter Olivia have been hugely patient and understanding that I shall be away this weekend – again. Dawn has been an outstanding single parent for so many weekends it is not true, and Olivia has become accepting of Daddy's odd lifestyle and time spent at his computer.

I'll just be five more minutes, I promise . . .

The author, David Addison, in the Silverstone commentary box at the 2022 British Grand Prix ready for another day of talking . . .

ABOUT THE AUTHOR

David Addison is a lifelong motorsport fanatic who has managed to make his hobby into a means of paying the bills.

As a commentator, David spent many years as the trackside voice at circuits around the UK as well as television coverage of national motorsport events. Since 2013 he has been ITV's lead commentator on the British Touring Car Championship and for SRO Motorsports Group headed the commentary for its myriad championships and races in the UK, mainland Europe, China, Japan, Malaysia and South Africa. He has covered Le Mans for Eurosport, V8 Supercars in Bahrain for Channel 7 and many of the Goodwood events as well as rallycross, truck racing and is the lead commentator each year for the British Grand Prix at Silverstone. A one-off outing competing in a Mini in 2000 convinced him that he was no racing driver.

A spell in the real world as press officer for the Manchester Chamber of Commerce and Industry honed David's ability to write as well as talk and since 2000 he has been a regular contributor and columnist for *Motorsport News* as well as its equivalent in Australia for a time.

An obsession with Alfa Romeos has recently been matched with one for Porsches and there is an increasing number both on the driveway and in the model cabinet, although there remains room for one more . . .

A proud member of the British Racing Drivers' Club, David lives in Cheshire. He has a wife and one daughter, who have an interest in motorsport but have remained able to keep it the right side of his obsession. This is his first book.

ALSO BY
GELDING STREET PRESS

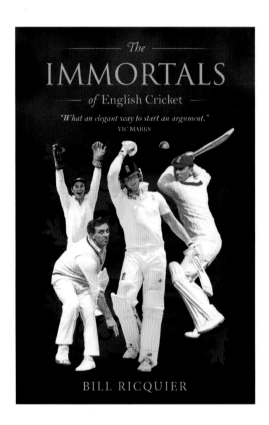

The Immortals of English Cricket

by Bill Ricquier

ISBN: 9781925946123